ACROSS
NEW MEXICO

A WANDERER'S GUIDE

Jill Schneider

Photography by D. Nakii

University of New Mexico Press
Albuquerque

Library of Congress Cataloging-in-Publication Data

Schneider, Jill, 1950–
    Route 66 across New Mexico: a wanderer's guide/
Jill Schneider; photography by D. Nakii. — 1st ed.
        p.   cm.
    Includes index.
    ISBN 0–8263—1280–2
    1. New Mexico—Description and travel—1981– —Guide-books.
    2. United States Highway 66—Guide-books.
    3. New Mexico—History, Local.
    4. Automobile travel—New Mexico—Guide-books.
    I. Title.
    II. Title: Route sixty-six across New Mexico.
    F794.3.S34   1991
    917.8904'33—dc20   91-12599

Designed by Joanna Hill.
Cartography by Michael Taylor.

CONTENTS

MAPS

Publisher's Note: The maps in this book are intended for general reference only. Although every effort has been made to ensure accuracy, we recommend that all wandering be done in consultation with an up-to-date, detailed road map of New Mexico.

CAVEAT EMPTOR

Don't put all of your faith in this book. It's largely memories; some are my own and some belong to other people. I can't claim that everything in this book is true. Memories are notoriously inaccurate, and wanderers are notorious storytellers. I don't think there are many outright lies in these pages. Most of the stories are the way people thought events occurred or the way they heard about them. You can't profitably debate truth with someone else's memories.

You can put your faith in the places described in this book. Every place mentioned here actually did exist on old Route 66. You can start out today and visit them, or what's left of them.

There are possibly more important sites along old Route 66. There are some that may have more historical significance. I've written only about the people and places and memories that matter to me. Those other important places are probably out there, somewhere. Go and find them. Perhaps you will end up with memories that matter to you.

HOW TO USE
THIS BOOK

This book is divided into three parts.

Part 1 takes you from Fourth Street and Central Avenue in Albuquerque west to the Arizona Border.

Part 2 directs you eastward from the Fourth Street and Central intersection in Albuquerque to the eastern boundary of New Mexico.

Part 3 tells the story of "older 66" and how Governor A.T. Hannett, reportedly in a fit of political pique, changed the direction of the highway.

You don't have to be a wanderer to use this book. You can stay home and read it and get pleasure from the stories and memories of other people. But if you are not an armchair traveler, get in your car, put the book in the glove compartment and drive out onto Interstate 40. When you see a mountain or a town or a twisting dirt road that intrigues you, get the book out. Whatever caught your eye might be in here.

Most of the places you can visit along old 66 can be reached by paved roads. However, you can take side trips away from the main path, and some of these may be excursions on dirt roads. The seasoned wanderer and outdoorsperson can skip the next few sentences of advice.

When you take to the dirt roads in New Mexico, you should include a shovel, a canteen of water, and a few matches in your gear. There aren't many road problems that can't be solved by digging. If you do get stuck and you can't dig out in a reasonable time, quit trying. If it's getting dark, use those matches to build youself an evening fire. This will lift your spirits. In the morning, take the canteen and start walking back to the highway to get help. End of advice.

The side trips are all marked on the maps with stars. Some of them are described in the book, and some of them are left for you to explore by yourself. All of the places you can go to on a side trip were at one time dependent on a flow of supplies coming down Route 66.

Much of the material in this book comes from the stories I heard from an old man I met in the bar at the La Posada Hotel in Albuquerque. He traveled up and down old Route 66 for a long time and did quite a bit of living along the old highway. His memories appear in a different typeface throughout the book. I would never have started the book if he hadn't told me those tales. I'm sorry that he checked out before the book was printed.

If you are a Wanderer at heart, you probably won't want or need a guide book. You will figure out where to go on your own. That's the essence of wandering.

Wandering has never been a high-status occupation in hard-working, hard-driven, ambitious America. Unless you were one of the few who brought back from some expedition the location of the Cumberland Gap or the way to the Northwest Passage, or gold, treasures, and jewels, wanderers weren't accorded much prestige.

They tell me that my great grandfather used to leave his farm chores undone and follow the honeybees into the woods. Sometimes he was gone all day, just wandering about. They say he never amounted to much.

Wanderers make their own trails, their own adventures and ultimately, their own books, published, and unpublished. This one is mine. I hope you enjoy it and better yet, I hope it leads you away from my paths and experiences and onto your own.

PREFACE

I would like to thank the people who helped me write this book. Some of them told me true stories; some of them told me lies. Some of them gave me money; some of them gave me time and memories. Some of the memories were as clear as on the day the events happened; some of the memories were worn by time. Some of the stories that I heard I did not include in this book, but hearing them helped me get a feel for Route 66 when it was the main highway across the United States.

This book is dedicated to the spirit of the Peddler, who showed me the Road and made me see it as it was. Without his memories, this book would not have been possible.

INTRODUCTION:

THE PEDDLER

"It's not the same." The old man spoke softly as he gazed at the high ceiling and painted beams in the hotel lobby. "It's close, but it's not the same."

We sat in the lobby of the La Posada Hotel in downtown Albuquerque. The La Posada had once been one of Conrad Hilton's splendid hotels. In fact, he had married Zsa Zsa Gabor in this particular hotel. But the Albuquerque Hilton had run down like an old clock, as had many grand hotels in many deteriorating downtowns. It had been quietly closed and its furnishings auctioned off. Then as the downtown revived, a new owner had come on the scene, tracked down the old furniture, and restored the old queen to a new splendor.

But the old man repeated, "It's nice but not the same. Not like the other times. Not like when it was *the* hotel on Route 66."

I encouraged him to tell me about the "other times." He had been a traveling salesman, a peddler, he called himself, and the towns along Route 66 in New Mexico had been his territory and the Hilton had been one of his places when he came to Albuquerque. He began to recount how Albuquerque's powerful and not necessarily rich used to gather at the old Hilton and shape the course of the city and the state. Names rolled off of his tongue: Clyde Tingley, the 1940s mayor, Licho Martinez, the political boss of one of the barrios, Donahoo, the first

Times change. Looking for old 66 along Interstate 40, west of Albuquerque. Nothing stays the same.

Gringo sheriff of Bernalillo County, all the shysters from the Buckhorn Poolhall on North Second, Jimmy O'Connor of the Little Theater. And Ramsey. Ramsey who owned the shoeshine parlor in the foyer of the Buckhorn Poolhall. A most respected colored man, a gentleman who owned his own home on First Street and who knew every person in town, even the kids. Ramsey who would loan a kid fifteen cents to go home on, and the kid would always pay the money back the next day. An extraordinary man.

"Not many of them were born in Albuquerque, but most of them came to town, down old Route 66. It was exciting then. The people and places were different in those days. There was so little television, well damn, there wasn't any television and little enough radio and not many movies or magazines giving you ideas. People made their own ideas. Ideas were different, too. There was more room to be more colorful, larger than life, more wicked, more virtuous. It took longer for the events of your past to catch up with you. And that's an advantage that's gone. The old man's voice had a slightly sardonic shade, a hint of the sinister. "Traveling was better then. It was. Traveling along Route 66 used to be an adventure. There were always things happening and things to see. You could drive the highway and anywhere you might pull over, there would be tourist traps with live rattlesnakes and Indian weavers. People would be selling garden produce from roadside stands or maybe genuine Indian pottery. Oh! That pottery! Those Indians would have great big bowls for sale. Big bowls all painted up with fancy designs, not like the dinky little pots you see today. And there would be hitch hikers and broken down cars and people camping out on the roadside. There was always something to see before the big trucks took over the road. As long as the railroads were still hauling freight, the road belonged to the travelers. You could stop at a small cafe, a family-run place and get a plate of real, blue corn-meal enchiladas and find out about the local dances and cockfights. People were more open then, and they were glad to see the traveler.

And the towns were so alive! Route 66 went right through Tucumcari and Santa Rosa and Albuquerque. It was the main street of Grants and it passed right through Gallup. You couldn't bypass any of the little towns like Logan or Moriarty, Correo, Cubero, or Budville. And things were happening in those little towns. You could see people going in and out of the stores and hotels and buildings. You could see wagons and teams on the streets with the cars and trucks. The highway went right through the middle of Laguna Pueblo and Paraje. The Indians lived right on the side of the road. It was so exciting to be stopped on Route 66 by a herd of sheep. It happened all of the time. You would be on this great highway, the highway that crossed America, and some shepherd carrying a goatskin canteen with the hair still on it would decide to cross his sheep and all of the traffic would stop for those sheep. The Interstate misses all of that now. Of course, the economy was different, too. It was around World War II times and things were booming. There was work and there was money. There were mines working near Gallup and there was a big truck farm at Grants and all of the Navajos were raising wool. Up in the northeastern part of the state they were building Conchas Dam. It was a good time to live. It was a good time to be traveling down Route 66. It can't all be gone. It can't all have vanished so fast."

The old man's voice had a wistful tone and he seemed to shrink into the big armchair. I couldn't stand it.

"Let's go!" I said and jumped out of the La Posada's elegant chair. "I want to see it! It's not gone! Not yet!" The old man brightened. He began to turn into the Peddler once again.

"I have to get my order book and grip," he announced firmly. He went over to the desk and retrieved a worn old suitcase and a black notebook. We went out to the curb to his grey '42 Packard.

"I'll drive," said the Peddler. "You don't know the road." His car smelled like leather and tobacco. We pulled around the corner to Third Street, went south a block and rolled onto old Route 66.

PART I

ALBUQUERQUE TO
THE ARIZONA BORDER

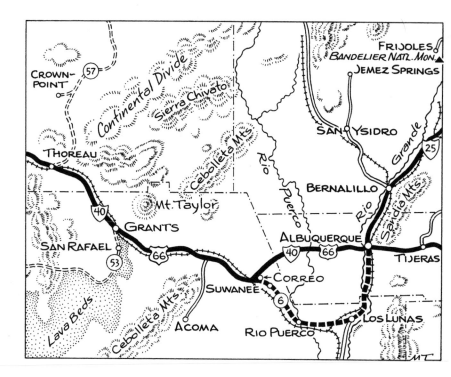

Map 1. Albuquerque to Grants (based on Roads to Cibola, New Mexico State Highway Commission, 1929).

1

ALBUQUERQUE

TO RIO PUERCO

WEST TO THE ALBUQUERQUE CITY LIMITS

Start at Fourth Street and Central in downtown Albuquerque and drive west on Central to the city limits. This is Route 66. In its days of glory Route 66 passed through the heart of Albuquerque and was the way west, out of town.

"In those days of early 66, Albuquerque wasn't much older than 66 itself. True, Albuquerque was originally settled early in the 1700s by the Spanish, but it didn't blossom into a bustling small town until the arrival of the railroad.

In the heyday of old 66, Albuquerque was small and everything was located downtown: the grocery stores, the furniture stores, the drug stores, the department stores as well as the doctors, lawyers, and city government. Somehow Albuquerque wasn't like other small towns. Albuquerque had class in a small and dusty way. It never had the 'wild west' history like some New Mexican towns such as Fort Sumner and Socorro. Instead it was a merchants' town, a family town, a safe, respectable place. Billy the Kid came to Albuquerque once, and was immediately thrown in jail. The old jail where he was locked up used to be on the corner of Central and Rio Grande Boulevard. It was only a few years ago that it was torn down and replaced with a car wash. Billy stayed in that jail for about two days, then he managed to escape. He got out of town and never came back. I always thought that someone missed a tourist trap opportunity there.

When I was traveling old 66, Albuquerque was a major stop and layover for the railroads. It had several big hotels for the travelers and a lot of people passed through Albuquerque, staying only a night or two. There was the Alvarado close to the railway station and the Hilton, the Cole, the Franciscan and the El Fidel. The Hilton was on Second Street, just off of 66, and on down Central there was the old and stately Franciscan at the corner of Sixth Street. The Franciscan had a uniformed doorman and a bellboy. It was a classy place for those times. If you went around the corner to Copper, you had the El Fidel. That old hotel had one of Albuquerque's first radio stations in the basement. Anyone could go down to the basement and watch the announcers and performers make the radio shows. The high school kids used to gather there in the late evenings to listen to the live performances.

In the evenings Albuquerque changed. All of the stores lining 66 had big brilliant neon signs and it was truly as light as day in downtown Albuquerque at night. When those signs would be lit up and flashing their jewel colors, then Albuquerque would lose some of its class and become lively and exciting and full of promise. I don't mean to say that it lost any of its safety and respectability; on any evening the streets of Albuquerque were filled with people. It was safe and pleasant to be on the street downtown and there was always something to do or somewhere to go. You could stop at the Kimo Cafe, next to the Kimo theater, and see all of the Class D baseball players, the farm team, eating a meal after a baseball game. Dorothea Caldwell would be there slinging hash and trading ribald remarks with the players and it was always a fun place to stop, late at night. The Court Cafe was the other late night restaurant in Albuquerque and you could always find someone there to tell you the news of the town."

As you drive through Albuquerque today, you will be able to find only a few of the Peddler's landmarks. The Franciscan Hotel, the El Fidel, and the Kimo Cafe are all gone. The old hotels have been replaced by other buildings and the Kimo Cafe is now the site of the Kimo Theatre Office. The Kimo Theatre itself, with its ornate facade and bright paint, has been turned into a small performing arts theater. When the Kimo was first erected its appearance caused some controversy among the citizens of Albuquerque. Some people thought its highly decorated exterior was a true representation of the spirit of the Southwest, while others thought it was a baroque monstrosity. Today you can simply say that there is no other building like it in the city.

Just before you reach the Kimo on Central you can spot Freed's on the north or right side of the street. If you like strange and rare objects, beads, oriental or Navaho rugs, sea shells, sheepskins, mechanical toys, Indian jewelry, or clothes from exotic places, you might want to visit Freed's. Freed's has all of these things and many more, and inventory changes constantly. The Freeds themselves will greet you with old-fashioned courtesy and answer any questions you may have regarding their treasure trove of merchandise. If you make a purchase they will wrap it up for you in brown paper and grocery string and send you on your way with a small gift of hard candy and a pleasant word.

After an arduous shopping trip at Freed's, stop next door at Capo's Deli for a late breakfast or a reviving snack. If the old road is pulling you on, take your order to go and head on down Route 66.

Going west on 66, you will soon come to the Manzano Day School. The brown adobe complex includes one building that was not intended for a school but was always known as an educational place. The structure on the east side of the campus was once the home of Billy Friday's Sunset Inn. It was a popular dinner and dance club for the pacesetters of Albuquerque. In the words of Gloria Mallory, present headmistress of the Manzano Day School, "Many a dance I danced with a sweaty-palmed youth, in the old Sunset Inn. Ah, what a place that was. What good times we had!"

When you reach the intersection of San Pasqual and Central, look to your left and spot the Albuquerque Little Theater. The Little Theater was a WPA project started in the early 1930s. Originally, the front of the building was decorated with an enormous mural depicting the New Mexico Civil War Battle of Glorietta. The artistic connection between a Civil War battle and a small-town performing arts theater is not clear. Anyone who has ever participated in community art productions however, may know about civil wars.

A theater is more than a building. Albuquerque was fortunate when Kathryn Kennedy O'Connor came to town and began the process that converted the empty stage into a theater. Kathryn O'Connor was a New York actress who left the Broadway stage and came to Albuquerque for her health. A woman with considerable talent and energy, the theater was what she knew best.

Under her direction, the Little Theater began to thrive, and people from all parts of Albuquerque began to take an interest in what was happening in the small building out on San Pasqual Avenue. Businessmen, teachers, lawyers, and laborers were all welcome participants in the productions. Kathryn Kennedy O'Connor tried to imbue them with the sense of professionalism that had helped make her a success on the Broadway stage.

"I remember that woman so well. She was a small person, a short woman but one you could not ignore or forget. One winter I knew I was going to be spending a great deal of time in Albuquerque so I tried out for one of the plays being produced by the Little Theater. The role I got was a supporting one, not the lead, and the play was a comedy which I thought would be easier than 'serious Drama.' Turned out it was harder and sometimes pretty discouraging work. I remember the pep talk, the speech Miss O'Connor gave the cast on opening night. 'Give the audience their money's worth,' she told us. 'They may have been to dinner and had a few drinks, they may talk out loud during your best speech, but by God they paid for their ticket and they *showed up* so don't cheat them. Give them everything you can. Give them a fair shake for their sugar.' That was Kathryn Kennedy O'Connor's credo: Give them everything you can.

She worked under pretty harsh conditions in Albuquerque, if you compare her experiences here with her life in New York. The Albuquerque Little Theater was somewhat primitive in those times. I remember where was no bathroom for the male actors. Between the acts they would go outside through the stage door and when they returned, you could see small drops of moisture on their dusty boots. Practical people would have suggested that the actors use the public restrooms, along with the audience, but Miss O'Connor said it was not professional, to have the audience and the actors mingle during the show. It destroyed the illusion you were trying so hard to create."

The Albuquerque Little Theater building is much larger now. The battle scene is gone from the front and there is a men's room for the actors as well as a paved parking lot. If you want to know if the actors and actresses are giving the people a fair shake for their sugar, you'll have to get off 66 and attend one of their plays.

As you approach the next major intersection, Rio Grande Boulevard and Central Avenue, you will begin to see signs directing you toward the right or north, to a place called Historic Old Town, the site where the first thirteen Spanish families built their homes and founded Albuquerque in 1705. Like the Spanish towns they left in Europe, The Villa de Albuquerque was built around a central square with a church dominating one side of the plaza. The plaza and church still remain, and the jail that was once in the center of the square has been turned into a bandstand. The church is still in use and all the homes around the plaza have been converted into shops, galleries and restaurants. If you are ready for some touristing of this kind by all means drive over to Old Town. Route 66 will still be heading west when you return to the road.

From the corner of Rio Grande Boulevard and Central Avenue, you can see the car wash standing on the site of the old jail. Across the street, in the Old Town Shopping Center, is the site of the Old Town Society Hall.

"The Old Town Society Hall was a dance hall. Every Friday and Saturday night they had a band and the people would gather there to dance and socialize. The bands that played there specialized in mariachi music, corridas, and the old fashioned Spanish two-step. The music was loud and exuberant. You could drive by the dance hall on any Friday or Saturday night in the spring or summer and hear the music in the street. Through the open door the lights would stream and the passer-by could catch a glimpse of bright crepe paper streamers and the flash of gayly colored, swirling skirts. I escorted a few young ladies in those days, whose mothers would not let them attend the dances in the Old Town Hall. Some people thought it was not the place for proper young ladies although I danced with many well-chaperoned young ladies there. The Old Town Dance Hall was another victim of progress. They tore it down to build the shopping center. I don't know where people go to dance and flirt and mingle now."

Continue west down Central Avenue. This used to be the main tourist section of Albuquerque. Although there were places for the travelers to stop and rest all along old Route 66, the big hotels were downtown and the tourist courts or motels outside of the downtown area on the sections of 66 that entered and left Albuquerque. Many of these independently owned motels still remain. You will pass by the Safari Lodge, the Texas Ann, and the El Vado, just to name a few. Each one of them had a brilliant neon-lit entrance way with a flashing "Vacancy" sign, and each one of them had an owner with a story.

"My favorite hotelkeeper was Texas Ann. Ann was a blonde, tall Texan with diamonds set in her front teeth. She was a pleasant lady who ran a clean, family motel. I found it difficult to talk with her as my gaze always wandered to those flashing stones in her mouth. They mesmerized me. It was hard to conduct a polite conversation with Ann because I could not stop myself from staring at those diamonds. I often wonder if she had that effect on others."

Just beyond the Texas Ann, before you cross the Rio Grande, look to the south, or your left. You will see a long narrow body of water with dirt banks, a few ducks, and if it is a clear day, a few fishermen. This is called Tingley Beach. It does not fit most people's conception of a beach but in the late thirties, it did. Under the dynamic leadership of Mayor Clyde Tingley, the city of Albuquerque constructed a public bathing beach here, with a mile of white sand on either side of a large freshwater lagoon. The water was pumped in from the Rio Grande, filtered, and circulated out. It was not unusual for entire families to gather and spend the day swimming and picnicking on the sand of Tingley Beach. Just as Route 66 is a memory of another time, so is Tingley Beach.

Cross the bridge and drive on to the city limits. An old travel book from 1949, *The American Guide*, describes the surroundings along this part of 66 as "verdant farmlands and orchards of the Rio Grande Valley." Try to imagine the fields and trees as you pass the shopping plazas, gas stations, fast-food restaurants, and discount stores.

As you approach the outskirts of Albuquerque, you will see a long hill rising to the horizon. This is Nine Mile Hill. Some say it was named because it once was nine miles long, before the engineers straightened it out and paved it into a highway. This is a myth. Nine Mile Hill is nine miles from the geographic center of Albuquerque, named, like many places in New Mexico, by the distance it is from some other geographical point. To many Albuquerqueans, Nine Mile Hill has a special meaning. If you were traveling east and you reached the hill, you were almost home. If you were traveling west, reaching Nine Mile Hill meant you were actually gone . . . out of town.

"It used to be that if you were traveling east, you couldn't see any part of Albuquerque until you topped out on Nine Mile Hill. There was nothing to see, just empty mesas and reaches of sky. Then you climbed the road to the top of Nine Mile Hill and Albuquerque simply appeared as if out of the Void. You could look down at night and see the town strung out along the river, a string of twinkly little lights stretching away north and south, branching off from Route 66. Albuquerque would be a little cluster of lights surrounded by darkness. No lights on the Sandia mountains, no houses in the foothills. No streetlights lining the freeway east. Just a small circle of lights marking a small town of fifty or sixty thousand. A little further east, a little way down Nine Mile Hill, you could turn off the road into some sand dunes and low hills that also overlooked Albuquerque. That was the place to go if you were a young couple in love and had a car. It was a place to neck and cuddle. I imagine that a great many citizens of Albuquerque got their start in life there. It was so romantic to be surrounded by darkness with the town shining away below."

THE ROAD TO RIO PUERCO

From the outskirts of the city to Rio Puerco, you have a choice of three routes. You can follow the directions on the green signboards and be sucked onto Interstate 40 heading west, you can make a hard right turn, go over the freeway, and travel along a frontage road that parallels the interstate on its north side, or you can turn left at the Chevron station and ride down an unofficial frontage road that is along the south side of I-40. Each path has its advantages. The freeway route will take you directly and quickly to Rio Puerco. The other two ways have individual attractions.

THE SOUTH FRONTAGE ROAD

As you reach the top of Nine Mile Hill, you will pass an abandoned gas station on your right and come to a three-way intersection flanked by a Chevron Station on the left and a Diamond Shamrock station on the right. Turn left here to get onto the south frontage road. This section of pavement is an actual remnant of old Route 66. The road is narrow, uncomfortably so, exactly wide enough for two cars. Traveling on this section will give you the idea of what rolling along Route 66 was like. Old Route 66 was just like this: narrow with little or no shoulder, miles of highway without billboards or other signs of habitation. As you go down this road you will be crossing a dramatic landscape that has barely changed in hundreds of years. As you gaze across land that sweeps from horizon to horizon with only the wrinkle of a butte or an up-thrust rock to interrupt it, the phrase "wide open spaces" takes on a more intense meaning; it ceases to be a tired, old cliché. There is a natural grandeur here that even the railroad tracks and the barbed-wire fences do not disturb.

This road dead-ends before you reach Rio Puerco, so when you come to an underpass that goes under the interstate, turn right and go through the long cement tunnel. This will deliver you out onto the north frontage road and along to Rio Puerco. Drive a bit cautiously through the tunnel in case there should happen to be a cow or two in there. The local ranchers use this land, and the underpass is for the livestock as well as the people. Also, by driving slowly through the underpass, you will have a good opportunity to study the graffiti on the walls. Some of the spray-paint philosophers are worth reading.

THE NORTH FRONTAGE ROAD

At the top of Nine Mile Hill you will come to a three-way intersection. Turn to the right and follow the green highway signs that will direct you over the freeway and onto the frontage road, which will take you the eight miles to Rio Puerco.

Past the adobe factory, on the right, you will see Herrera Rancho, a neat fenced compound with a neat house. This is a private residence. I have heard the story that when someone asked Mr. Herrera why he lived where he did, surrounded by a chain-link fence that lent an unusual air to his estate, he simply commented that it was what he wanted to do.

Past the Herrera Estate, you will see a large group of buildings set well away from the road. They are difficult to miss because of the round structure that looks like a giant white ball floating among the buildings. This is an old radar site, abandoned by the U.S. Government. The site has had a checkered career since the federal government turned it over to the city of Albuquerque. In turn, it has been a rehabilitation center for substance abusers, a home for the homeless, and a monstrous headache to the city and the taxpayers alike.

If you are driving to Rio Puerco in the early fall, the land may be in bloom with yellow and purple wildflowers. As you look to the north you will be able to see great patches of yellow spread out on the land and along the deep ravine that marks out the course of the Rio Puerco. The Rio Puerco is not actually a river except by Southwestern definition. There are many times, in fact most of the time, when the Rio Puerco is a dry riverbed with no water at all. It turns into a river only after a rain, when the riverbed fills with water washing down from the land to the north, water that runs swift and treacherous into the Rio Grande. Then the Rio Puerco is a river. Its water will be silty and sandy and a deep rusty red, and will look like something you might associate with *puerco*, which is Spanish for "pig" and "dirty."

After passing the radar site, you can see I-40 begin to curve gently away to the left. Near this point, the frontage road begins to follow the original route of Highway 66.

RIO PUERCO

Today when you approach the place on the Puerco where the road crosses the river or the riverbed, depending on the weather, you will see gas stations and trading posts grouped on either side of the highway. This is Rio Puerco. Hundreds of years ago this area was inhabited by primitive people who ranged up and down this red ravine and left behind all manner of pottery and stone tools as evidence of their life along the river. You can still walk up and down almost any part of the Rio Puerco and pick up a pot shard or a stone graver. Many people who attended the University of New Mexico got their introduction to archeology along the sand stretches of the Rio Puerco.

Rio Puerco also used to be famous for its polar bear. Pull off the highway and into the Rio Puerco Trading Post and you would be met by a full-sized, adult Polar Bear. Stuffed. In a glass case. This was the last thing anyone ever expected to find in the New Mexico landscape. It was a trophy of a hunting trip to the Arctic and a reminder of everything that was not to be found along this part of Route 66. Sometimes the bear would be in the trading post and sometimes it would greet you out by the gas pumps. It was a part of Rio Puerco for so long that it was a well-known landmark all by itself. One night someone broke the case and spirited the stuffed bear away. It was later found on the east side of Albuquerque, high up in the Sandias, completely torn to pieces.

"That bear. Not everyone thought he was so great. There are other people living around Rio Puerco besides gas station attendants and tourists. The Cañoncito Navaho Indian Reservation is just about seven or eight miles away. The Indians see bears differently than white people do. They don't stuff them and they don't talk about them except at appropriate times. Bears can be powerful. A wise person doesn't fool around with power frivolously. All it would take would be someone's sheep dying or children getting sick and someone might decide that the polar bear, the White Bear, wasn't happy in that case and someone might do something about it. Do something to make the bear happy, so that the sheep wouldn't die and the children would get well. Maybe set that bear free, maybe let him be really, truly dead like he was when he was shot. Not such a big mysterious thing. Not a crime. A release. A purification."

Inside the Rio Puerco Trading Post you will find all kinds of wonderful tourist junk from rubber tomahawks and rose pod sachets to some very tasteful silver jewelry. At the Rio Puerco Trading Post you can always get coffee, pop, and sandwiches to hold you over until the next stop.

Across the road is a franchised tourist stop, good old Stuckey's. If you are feeling ornery, this is a fine place to pick a fight with your traveling companions. Depending on where you grew up in the United States, this place will be called "Stookey's" or "Stuckee's." A debate over the correct pronunciation will last for miles unless you are traveling with children, in which case it might last forever. Think about this.

"See that fine old iron bridge there, spanning the Puerco? It sure was a boon to the traveler. It was only two lanes but it insured the fact that you could cross the river in any weather. Before that grand bridge was constructed there was only a single-lane span. When traffic was heavy on 66, the cars would line up on either side of that narrow thing and take turns crossing it. And before that, there was no bridge at all. The road just went down over the side of the ravine, across the riverbed, and up the other side. When it rained, you would be stuck on either side of the river. It wasn't just the unpredictable nature of the water that was the obstacle. It was the mud and the steep sides of the riverbank that stopped those old cars, too. The Indians would always show up with their teams after a rain and wait for the motorists. When a motorist realized that he couldn't cross the riverbed with his mechanized horsepower, the Indians would be there. For a sum of money, they would pull the car across with genuine horsepower. In a way it was like an ambush, a businesslike arrangement where the past took advantage of the present. Not such a bad deal."

RIO PUERCO TO

OLD LAGUNA VIA MARQUEZ

RIO PUERCO TO MARQUEZ

If you don't need to head west immediately, the side trip to Marquez from Rio Puerco can be a diverting adventure. On this trip you will be able to see some wild and empty land. Some will regard it as beautiful. Such vastness and lack of people are elements that are becoming something of a rarity in the twentieth century.

As soon as you cross the old iron bridge spanning the Rio Puerco on old 66, turn right. There will be signs directing you to the left and straight ahead but only one points right. This sign will read "Austra-Tex Oil Company." Take this road. You might want to write down your odometer reading in this space: _____ . Wanderers do not often trouble themselves with mileage but you might consider it for this trip. The next thirty-two miles are not highway miles and it might bring you some comfort to be able to cross-check your mileage with the landmarks and this book and confirm that you are on the road to Marquez. The way is not dangerous but in the words of Robert Frost, it is "the one less traveled by." It is not a tourist highway.

About a mile down the road, you will reach a cattleguard with a battered sign fastened to the fence, on the right. The sign says:

Wet, muddy adobe roads can be perilous.

Stay on the road
No hunting
No shooting
$500 fine

The sign and every fence post around it riddled with bullet holes. It doesn't take long, once you leave Highway 66, to get into the wide open spaces and encounter the great hostility and hospitality of the West.

The advice to stay on the road is good advice. If you are lucky, the road will have been graded in the last six months or so. This is not a bad road; almost any car can travel it. You should probably plan to drive slowly. If it is rainy or wet, bear in mind two of the Laws of the Road: (1) Wet sandy stretches of road are easy driving (2) Wet, muddy, adobe stretches of road can be perilous. You don't need a four-wheel-drive vehicle for these roads, just time.

Approximately six miles from the Rio Puerco turnoff, you will be able to see a ring of light-colored stones, off to the right side of the road. This is a ruin of an old Navaho dwelling or a hogan. You may or may not want to stop here.

Abandoned hogan is an excellent example of native stone construction.

The traditional Navahos, who probably built this place, rarely abandon a good hogan unless someone has died within its walls. Traditional Navahos hold the belief that death is a part of the natural cycle but one must be cautious around death. Death is death and life is life and the two are not mixed. If someone in the Navaho world is about to die, they are sometimes carried carefully outside of the hogan so that the rest of the family living there is not affected by death. The land can absorb death but a dwelling can be affected by *chindi*. This word does not translate easily into English. *Chindi* is similar to the memory of all of the negative aspects and bad deeds of the person who has died. It is not quite a metaphysical concept like a soul or a spirit, but it is something that is not good for the living. It is difficult to rid a place of *chindi*. It is better to move. If you are sensitive to this sort of thing, then drive on. If not, then stop and see some interesting, native stonework. Try to imagine what it would be like to live in this spot that is so close to metropolitan Albuquerque but seems so far away from it.

A short distance on you will see a road leading off to the left. It will be marked with a sign featuring a "58" superimposed on a large ar-

Just how big are the holes?

rowhead. This road leads to the Cañoncito Navaho Indian Reservation Chapter House. Do not take this road. Continuing, you will see a great white butte bulking up ahead, with what looks like a scattered settlement on the left. This collection of buildings and corrals is the home of an extended Navaho family. Such a family unit may be as large as twenty or thirty people.

The country here is rugged and wild. For all of mankind's power, it seems that this is a spot where we have not had too much impact. It is a bit too late now to wonder if you packed the shovel and canteen. If you forgot them, a twinge of anxiety is appropriate now. In this place, it's difficult to believe you had a hot restaurant breakfast just this morning, in Albuquerque. It's difficult to believe that Albuquerque even exists.

You are now traveling across land that belongs to the Cañoncito Navaho. If you should meet a cowboy in a pickup truck, it very likely will be Raymond Gonzales, who runs cattle on this land. Keep on the road. There will be branch roads going off to the left and right but you should be able to discern the main path. You can't get hopelessly lost here because all of the roads lead, if not to Rome, at least to SOME-

The sky is wide. The land is wide.

WHERE. Just keep driving and a road sign will eventually show up. If all else fails, consult the map on page 6 in the front of this book.

Square-topped mesas frame the world here. Huge towers that carry power lines take on the aspect of walking giants. The sky is wide. The land is wide. It takes a few scattered cattle or a truck down the road to bring perspective to the view.

Approximately sixteen miles from the departure point at Rio Puerco, you will come to a sturdy old bridge that is in decline. At this point you can balance safety against the Indiana Jones Method of Bridge Crossing. The Jones Method works like this: when faced with a questionable bridge, drive across it like a bat out of hell, betting that it will collapse behind you rather than in front of you. This always works in the movies. In reality, you might want to get out of your car, walk across the bridge, and see how big the holes in the bridge really are. Consider the road you have just driven over. Take into account the feelings of wrecker drivers who sometimes charge you according to

It takes a few cattle to bring perspective to a view.

their emotional state rather than some other rational scale. How decrepit is this bridge?

In the early fall this bridge will be surrounded with clouds of color. Tall globe mallows will be glowing orange. Purple asters will push up around the bridge approach. Salt cedars in the arroyo will be delicately tinted lilac. The snakeweek will be blooming yellow. You might want to gather some mallow, whose old Spanish name is *flor de la negrita.* Traditionally this plant has been used by the Hispanic people of the Southwest for a hair rinse and hair restorative. A note of caution: the old curanderas report that if the infusion of mallow is not rinsed completely out of your hair, you will end up with many small, tight curls.

If the flowers are decorating the old bridge, try for a photograph. Just snap the shutter and let the color processing company do the rest. Someone just like you probably made all of those souvenir postcards.

On the other side of the bridge are some unusual geological formations. Red-topped cliffs are underpinned with white foundations, and weirdly shaped mesas edge the landscape. High bluffs are covered with cracks that look like wrinkles in the skin or fine lines found in very old porcelain.

The road now is a true Wanderer's road. As you go through the hilly country spotted with stunted and twisted cedars, you will be treated to the sudden surprise of jagged rocks thrusting up through the mat of desert plants. Just when you are convinced that you have left civilization far behind, you will roll across a cattleguard and see to the left a corral and a loading chute. It is startling to be reminded that people are making a living off this isolated and desolate land.

Twenty miles from the Rio Puerco turnoff, you sould come up on a blue-and-gold Cibola County sign with a "3" on it. If you find this sign, you are on the road. About a mile further on, the power lines will leap up to the top of a beautiful, triple-tiered, square-edged mesa. The road will be following a deep, rugged arroyo. Watch the arroyo and as it begins to curve away from you and lead to the right, you should be able to spot a leafy, non-desert tree growing incongruously on the inner wall of the arroyo. Only a very tough tree, a determined life form, could establish itself in this hostile environment and fourish. This non-native tree exists only because the curve of the arroyo collects excess moisture from the sporadic rains. That tree may not command your respect, but it does command your attention.

If you look now to your left, you can see Fortress Hill. This interestingly, cone-shaped hill with square battlements resting on its shoulders is not man-made although its symmetry suggests it.

Approximately two miles beyond the hardy tree in the arroyo you will pass another Cibola County sign. This one is on the opposite side of the road, facing away from you. Twist around in your seat and make sure it reads "2." You are on the right road to Marquez. Soon you will come to another sign restricting the speed limit to forty-five miles per hour. This looks like an official State of New Mexico road sign. Considering the condition of the road, you have to believe that someone in the State Highway Department has a rare or crude sense of humor. Or maybe someone *not* with the Highway Department, has a quirky sense of the absurd.

In this area you will see a prolific growth of cholla cactus. These are the tall branching cacti with slender arms. Their skin is green and they produce yellow flowers that give way to bright yellow, flower-

A rugged cholla grows out of a tiny rock fissure in a classic desert environment.

shaped fruit. Beneath the prickly green skin, the cholla has a firm skeleton-like inner structure. When the cholla dies, and the green, moisture-laden parts of the plant dry away in the sun, the inner skeleton is revealed, a woody support system that looks very much like expanded metal lath rolled into a cylinder. This is the cactus of walking sticks, lamps, and souvenirs in tourist traps all over the Southwest. It is hard to resist picking up some of the perforated wood and taking it home and putting in with all of the other stuff you plan to "make into something, someday."

As you are rolling along, look to your right. Far in the distance you should be able to see Cabezon Peak rising tall and blue among the earth-toned hills and mesas. Cabezon Peak is a 2,200-foot-high volcanic plug or a giant blob of lava that oozed up from below the earth's surface. In recent times, Cabezon Peak has been regarded as an outstanding landmark for airplane pilots. Before that it was a step on a stagecoach route. It also has an even more ancient history. According to the Navahos, at the time when people had just arrived in this world,

This desert denizen and Cabezon Peak (background) remain unchanged despite human efforts in this harsh land.

the land was inhabited by many cruel and unusual monsters. Two young men, twin brothers with divine origins, were sent to make the world safe for the Navahos. The pair used magical weapons and cunning traps to destroy the monsters who were preying on the people. Cabezon Peak is regarded by the Navahos as the head of one of the monsters destroyed by the twins. Interestingly enough, *cabezon* is the Spanish word for "big head." The early Spanish explorers and exploiters were not especially tolerant of Indian culture, so it is somewhat of a mystery why this name continued. The culturally ethnocentric Spanish had a tendency to put their own labels on places in the New World.

SIDE TRIP TO THE KERR-MCGEE MINE

Begin to watch for a road that turns off the right. You should find it approximately twenty-five miles from your original starting point at the Rio Puerco. This road will take you on a side trip to the unopened, unworked, yet completely established, Kerr-McGee uranium mine. If you are amused at the schemes of the rich and powerful gone awry, this trip could entertain you. If you like to see human endeavor, you could see that also. If you are a sightseer, this uranium mine is an interesting site.

As you bump over this road you will be struck by a juxtaposition of the old and the new. Power lines cross this country, sharing the land with stock corrals. Although we are living in an age where technology has harnessed the power of uranium, we are still obtaining food from animals that roam the land, grazing on wild plants.

After you pass a stock corral, the road will fork. Take the right fork. The road will begin to widen out and become flatter. It is no longer a track but more like a road. You will notice that now it is going through deep cuts in the hillsides, instead of crawling over hills. The Kerr-McGee Company engineered this road to accommodate heavy machinery as well as hundreds of workers. Soon you will reach a fence that guards an array of buildings. The mining company came to this isolated spot and established offices, changing rooms, workshops, and maintenance areas to support the business of mining uranium. A mine shaft was drilled, and made ready for the miners. Work was planned for several hundred people. By the time everything was ready to start production, the uranium boom was busted. No one was ever called to work in this mine. It is said that the mine has filled up with water.

This Kerr-McGee site is a lonely and desolate place. The wind never seems to stop blowing. Occasionally a caretaker visits and checks on the property. To me, this place is a reminder of how fragile and puny mankind's efforts can be. Human beings sought to subdue the land, mine the uranium and reap the profit. In the end, those efforts came to nothing but unused facilities. The square-topped mesas and faraway Cabezon Peak remain as they were when humanity began its frail efforts here.

In the end, human effort came to nothing but unused facilities.

Turn around and drive back the way you came. Turn right, back onto the road you were previously following and keep on it until you come to a very wide, well-maintained, graveled highway. Finding this clear, broad road is a shock after traveling the rutted, twisted roads of the last twenty-nine miles. This is Laguna road or New Mexico 279. Turn right here. In approximately four miles, you will find a sign commanding you to stay on the main road by order of the Juan Tafoya Land Corporation. Since it's the corporation's road from her to Marques, it's a do-it-or-else situation. In fact, anything else and you are trespassing on private property. About a mile on you will climb a short hill, and behold Marquez, New Mexico. Population: not too many. Condition: ghostly.

MARQUEZ

The road before you will take you down into Marquez proper. The road to the right will lead to the Long Island Lighting Company (LILCO)

What will you find in Marquez? ¿Quien sabé? Go and look.

uranium processing plant and rolling mill, while the road to the left leads to the LILCO uranium mine. Both the mill and the mine are closed, still more victims of the uranium bust. According to Bud Gunderson of Grants, LILCO is known in the East because the customers of this power company have been in long litigation to avoid paying for the mine and processing plant at Marquez.

Marquez, your goal, is before you. A privately owned town, it was named for the Marquez family who founded it and lived in the area for many years. The heirs of the family now own it. It is difficult to predict what you will find if you go down to visit Marquez. On different visits I have found different kinds of welcomes. Once I was chased away by a hostile inhabitant who didn't want me taking pictures of the church. I have also been greeted by playing children, and have dri-

The church at Marquez.

ven through Marquez when I would've sworn it was a ghost town—completely deserted.

There are few signs of the new in Marquez. Here and there you can see new mobile homes nestled down among the old adobe walls. A shiny pickup may be parked outside a home with a TV antenna. The church usually looks like no one is caring for it. Marquez is an enigma. What will you find? Quien sabe? Go and look.

You used to be able to leave Cuba, New Mexico and drive to Marquez over the back roads. From Marquez you could travel on to Laguna and then depart to Albuquerque or Grants or Gallup. I have not been able to do this in recent years. Drive as I might around Marquez, all I can find are padlocked gates barring the way to the roads leading north. I have left Cuba and started south to Marquez and have encountered the padlocks on the gates there, too. Times change.

Leave Marquez and begin the trip to old Laguna. You will be travelling back on the same road, New Mexico 279, that you used for the last leg of the journey to Marquez, and you can travel most of the way to Old Laguna by this route. Spinning down this broad graveled road you might begin to feel a bit uneasy, even a bit outraged. Is it true, is it possible that you could have driven almost all of the way to Marquez on this smooth and pleasant highway? Could you have reached Marquez without enduring the ruts, the bumps and the dust? Yes!

Along 279, you can see many high, flat-topped mesas that are characteristic of the Southwest landscape. Their stair-stepped silhouette of these mesas is a design motif frequently used by Native American artists in jewelry, baskets, and rugs, a common motif no matter which tribe the artists claim as their people. If you should ever meet one of these artists and be brash enough to ask if their design is representative of the high mesas, you will probably get one of these five possible answers: (1) Yes (2) No (3) It's a cloud (4) It's a traditional design (5) What do the designs on your tie mean? Whatever the answer, it seems likely that the dramatic landscape and the strong lines in the Southwestern environment would play some part in influencing an artist who grew up in this part of the world.

The land on either side of the road here is covered with small, round bushes. The leaves of this plant are also small and dull. This little plant is unimpressive. These are not flamboyant desert flora. These little bushes are snakeweed, *escoba de la vibora*, or Gutierrezia, depending on whether the observer is a rancher, an herbalist, or a botanist. Many traditional stockmen of the Southwest believe that snakeweed springs up on land that has been over-grazed. If a pregnant cow cannot find other forage and eats too much snakeweek, spontaneous abortion is a possible result. Curanderas or herbalists know that *escoba de la vibora* is a useful plant for relieving the pain of arthritis. It has been used in New Mexico for this complaint for hundreds of years. Botanists recognize snakeweed as Gutierrezia, a member of the composite family. In the fall, snakeweed bears yellow blossoms and covers the ground like long spills of bright yellow paint.

About ten miles from Marquez, you will begin to notice that something is horribly wrong with the land. The vegetation (such as it is) begins to dwindle and become ragged and stunted. You are in the vi-

Spare vegetation, ragged and stunted, surrounds the uranium tailings.

cinity of a dump where the waste material or tailings from a uranium mine were discarded. The mine is closed now, but the effect it had on the land remains. The Environmental Protection Agency assures us that this place is perfectly safe.

SEBOYETA

Seboyeta is the first town you will come to after leaving Marquez. Highway 279 appears to intersect with another road here. In reality, 279 makes a sharp turn to the left and heads southward. If you turn right, you will be able to tour the town of Seboyeta.

Seboyeta is Spanish for "a place with many onions"; less elegantly, *seboyeta* mans "oniony." The correct Spanish spelling of this is *cebolleta* but life and history are full of inexactitudes.

Seboyeta looks like a small, quiet New Mexican town. As you drive around the dusty roads, you will see adobe homes with tin roofs, mobile homes with added-on porches, horse trailers, and pickup trucks. There is also a post office, a church, a tennis court, and a basketball court. Horses graze along the roadside. Dogs bark at strangers. It seems pleasant and entirely tranquil.

The history of Seboyeta is anything but tranquil. At the end of the eighteenth century, a group of thirty families was attempting to settle and farm the land surrounding present-day Seboyeta. During this time, the Navahos were not peaceful, nomadic Shepherds, but were instead a rather aggressive group who were trying to wrest the same land away from the Pueblo Indians. Apparently when the Spanish Crown gave the land to the Spanish settlers, those in the Spanish throne room did not take into account the fact that the indigenous peoples might have some strong feelings of ownership. Times were tense around the Seboyeta area, no matter which interest group one belonged to.

In 1804, a wall ten feet high was built around Seboyeta. The thirty farming families would take refuge behind this wall whenever the previous inhabitants of the land threatened them. At one time, the newcomers were held behind the wall by five thousand Navahos. After driving through Seboyeta today and seeing the lack of inhabitants in the area, one wonders what it would be like to see five thousand people in Seboyeta, not to mention five thousand Indians intent on changing the hearts and minds of thirty farming families. Remnants of the wall can still be seen in the town.

BIBO

Beyond Seboyeta a few miles you will come to Bibo. You will know you are there when you pass A. A. Michaels Bar and Restaurant on the right side of the road. Bibo was a trading post in the early 1900s, named for the family that settled there and ran the trading post. Some members of the Bibo family are still living in this part of New Mexico.

As you travel away from Bibo, you will see a huge, strange, stair-stepped mesa far away to your left. When you draw closer you will see that this is not a natural geologic formation. It is instead the overburden from the Jackpile Open Pit Uranium mine. This is the material that was removed so that the miners could get at the uranium-bearing sandstone below. The Jackpile mine was named for Jack Knaebel, a

Man-made mesas: overburden from the Jackpile Open Pit Uranium Mine.

mining engineer and geologist. When the Jackpile was in operation, it was the largest open-pit uranium mine in the United States. A great many people moved a great deal of earth here. The Anaconda Company paid good wages and many men and women learned the skills associated with uranium mining. The mine is located on Laguna Reservation land and the tribe was paid millions of dollars in royalties. The mine is no longer in operation and the Laguna Indians have received more dollars to form their own company, move the dirt, and reclaim the land.

Keep on 279 until it meets Highway 124. Turn left here. You are once more on a strip of old Route 66. This section of 66 went right by the Laguna Indian Pueblo. To see old Laguna, continue east on 124. Just before you reach a gas station on the right, turn right. You should see a post office on your left. Old Laguna is straight ahead, resting on the hill in front of you.

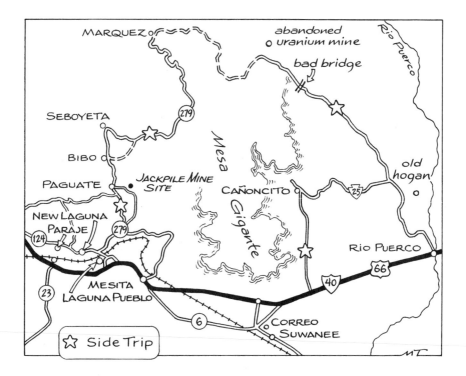

Map 2. *Side Trip: Rio Puerco to Old Laguna via Marquez.*

RIO PUERCO TO
OLD LAGUNA VIA CORREO

RIO PUERCO TO CAÑONCITO

If you don't want to spend your time wandering around the hinterlands going to Marquez, or if it is raining, stay on I-40 out of Rio Puerco and drive west to Old Laguna. The scenery on this drive is superb if not overwhelming. If you like space and drama, this is your country. The land has been described many ways, but no one ever called it tame.

One-and-a-half miles from Rio Puerco, look to your right and try to spot an off-white outcropping of stone that looks oddly worn away. This is a variety of a very soft volcanic rock known as tuff or tufa. The Navaho silversmiths use this soft material to make the type of jewelry known as "sandcast silver."

A silversmith desiring to make some sandcast silver first goes to some spot where he has seen an outcropping of tufa. Using an ordinary wood saw, he quarries some of this soft stone. Later, in his workshop, he will carve into the tufa a negative of the piece of jewelry he has in mind. He then pours molten silver into this mold. When the metal is cold, the artist files and polishes and works the silver to completion. Since the tufa molds are very fragile, they can rarely be used more than once. Thus each piece of sandcast silver is truly unique.

Today, technology and scarcity are changing the methods of the traditional silversmith. Sandcast jewelry is being made in molds carved from cuttlebone (the same material that is placed in birdcages for parakeets), firebrick, and other high-tech materials. If you want to determine if this piece of jewelry has been cast in a tufa mold, look at the reverse side and check for a textured surface. The rough, sand-grain surface is not always smoothed away on the old and traditional pieces of jewelry.

This particular outcropping of tufa is on Laguna Indian land. It has been quarried by many silversmiths and is nearly gone.

Past the tufa outcropping old 66 will be running parallel to I-40 on the north. As you drive along, the interstate will occasionally swerve slightly and swallow up chunks of the original roadbed. Between the interstate and the frontage road, however, you will have a good general idea of where the old highway went. You may travel on the frontage road for a space but it does deadend at a gate leading to the Pueblo Laguna land. At this point you must turn around and go back and get on I-40.

CAÑONCITO

Thirteen miles from Rio Puerco, Exit 313 will announce the Cañoncito turnoff. (Cañoncito is pronounced can-yon-see-toe, although many people say can-yon-chee-toe.) Take this road if you wish to visit one of the four Navaho Indian Reservations in New Mexico. There are nine places in New Mexico named Cañoncito and every one of them is in, or by, a little canyon (*cañoncito*).

The Cañoncito Navaho are a small band. They have a day school and a chapter house in this rather isolated spot outside of Albuquerque, north of old 66. I don't know how or why they separated from the other larger groups of the Navaho. I imagine it's an interesting story.

The Cañoncito Navaho Reservation may appear to be a severe and even forbidding locale but like most communities, the beauty of the place is in the people, not the physical location. The Cañoncito Navahos demonstrated their inner beauty after the Cañoncito tornado, which also earned the reservation a place in New Mexico meteorological history.

This is what happened: In the early 1980s, a tornado touched down in Cañoncito and tore the roof from a mobile home and generally wrought all kinds of destruction. This was a very traumatic event because a tornado is one of those things that is Not Supposed to Happen in the Middle of New Mexico. Before the Cañoncito Tornado, you could have asked any number of weatherpeople about the possible danger of tornados in the middle of New Mexico and they would have all said "No sweat. No danger. Never happen there. No tornados in the middle of New Mexico." And then they would have all smiled.

After the Cañoncito Tornado, there was a great deal of media attention. After that died away, repairs were made to the damaged buildings. In many other places and other societies, that would have been that. But the Cañoncito Navahos knew that wasn't the end of their ordeal. They knew they had to do one more thing before the tornado would really be over. They got in touch with a singer, a *hatali*, and had a ceremony to ease the minds of the people who had been troubled by this terrible disaster. In the traditional Navaho way, they restored the inner community as well as the outer, physical one.

CORREO

Slightly past the Cañoncito exit, Interstate 40 deviates from the path of old 66. The old highway used to take off to the south here, heading toward a place known as Correo. Look across the land to your left or south and you can discern a faint but unmistakable track leading away from the Interstate, across the country. That is old 66.

Correo used to be right on Route 66, a little town of nothing more than a gas station, a bar-restaurant, a post office, and a tourist court. The post office opened in 1914 and was the only spot for miles around where you could receive mail. *Correo* is the Spanish name for mail, which actually came to the railroad stop about four miles southeast of Correo. This stop on the Atchison, Topeka, and Santa Fe Railroad was originally called San Jose, but railroad company officials changed that name to Suwanee when they realized there was another San Jose on the same line in Oklahoma.

To visit Correo, take the Los Lunas exit, Exit 126, and drive onto New Mexico State Road 6. Turn left at the sign advertising the Wild Horse Mesa Bar. This strip of blacktop is old 66 again. The place known as Correo is gone, although you can drive down the old highway, which is now choked with weeds, until you come to a locked gate. Old 66 is still intact, striking over the desert toward Albuquerque. You can see it beyond the barbed-wire fence, its edges blurred by the encroaching weeds. Soon the desert will cover it entirely.

Before the advent of the Wild Horse Mesa Bar and after the construction of I-40, you could drive out to this spot and see the remains of Correo. You would find a string of concrete slabs neatly lined up

Old 66, choked with weeds and without travelers, heads east to Albuquerque from Correo.

under the New Mexico sky. Each of the slabs was covered with a black and white checkerboard of linoleum tiles. Each of the checkerboard slabs had at one time been the floor of a tiny tourist room at the Correo Tourist Court. The black and white squares were an oddly rigorous pattern among the soft lines of the desert. Those concrete slabs are in a dump behind the bar now, and nothing remains of the little place called Correo but a power pole. It is hard to imagine that this was once a welcoming stop along old Route 66.

Retrace your path back to New Mexico 6, cross it, and head westward. This is another section of old 66. You have to drive over an aging overpass that arches above the railroad tracks. As you go west, you will see a cluster of ruined and crumbling buildings, all abandoned now. Just over the bridge is an old building decorated with a painting of a black-and-white Indian rug. The painting is on the wall that faced old 66. This is all that's left to entice tourists off the highway and into the building. It is interesting to note how close the buildings were to the road. There were no quarter-acre parking lots in those times. There were not enough cars on the road to warrant such an arrangement.

As you drive down the narrow blacktop, you can get a very realistic idea of what Route 66 was like in the forties. It is empty and quiet, unlike the continual whiz and roar of the modern four-lane. There is nothing man-made here but the road and the car. It is easy to imagine how a trip across the country on Route 66 might have been daunting to the timid. Driving across the country at that time was an adventure. There was really nothing and nobody for miles and miles. The sight of a passenger or a freight train was a happy indicator of the other people and other places.

The road is severely rutted and in some places there are potholes but it is very drivable. It gets better the farther west you go. Approximately one-and-a-half miles from the old overpass, New Mexico 55 turns south and goes off to the Alamo Navaho Indian Reservation. This band of Navahos is known to some people as the Rock Eaters but that is another tale and another trip.

If you have been grumbling about or merely noticing the primitive condition of the road, think about this: until 1937, Route 66 was unpaved. The major highway across one of the most powerful countries in the world was dirt. Americans had Packards, Fords, Chevrolets, DeSotos, Hudsons, Chryslers and Studebakers. What they didn't have was a paved road so that they could drive their marvelous collection of automobiles in comfort from coast to coast.

In the early 1920s work began on a completely paved, two-lane transcontinental highway that would stretch from Illinois to California. This road would be Route 66. It was built in sections, rather than as one continuous job, and as work was planned for each part, word was passed through the communities concerned and muleskinners would begin to show up with their teams. It was muleteams that pulled the graders, levelers, and packers used to build the roadbed, mules and men who accomplished most of the actual construction of this road. It seems ironic that a road built for automobiles would be built by muscle and sweat rather than gas-powered machines.

Scattered along the old road are small abandoned buildings and houses that are slowly turning into memories. Take time to pull over at one of these small spots that mark some human endeavor and get out and walk around. If you are sharp-eyed, you may be able to find a piece of glass turned purple by the sun or a rusty bottlecap. You can try to imagine what motivated people to come to one of these lonely places and build a home or run a business. The little stone ruins dot the hills. Was this a small community? Did people live here all at the same time? Or is it a story of individuals who came, stayed for awhile, and then moved on? Although the wide land and the big sky appeal to some, they must have been fierce and unwelcoming to others.

When you see a group of industrial buildings on your left, you will be passing a natural gas compression station. Ahead and to your right is one of the Pueblo Laguna towns called Mesita. Stay on the road. It will curve about and take you to the frontage road next to Interstate 40. This frontage road covers sections of old Route 66 and also parts of the bypass that was built to carry traffic while I-40 was under construction. It will give you a great feel for the way old 66 swung through the landscape, rather than plowing straight across it. The frontage road curves to miss the great red butte, as old Route 66 did; Interstate 40 cuts through the red cliffs.

"See that old arroyo going along near the road? I have driven here when the rain was falling and the water was washing up to the roadbed in that thing. You could get behind one of the little old semi-trucks they had then, who would be behind a model A Ford, who would be following a wagon and team driven by Indians. The rain would be pouring down, and we would all be creeping around these curves in the storm. The highway would be disappearing into the water and it would be dark and you wouldn't dare pass because of the traffic that might be coming the other way. Oh yes, I remember the stretch of 66 around Mesita."

Soon you will be approaching Old Laguna. From the highway or the frontage road, Old Laguna is visible, sitting on a hill, its white church gleaming against the sky. Sometimes when the light is not bright, it is hard to see this cluster of houses on the hill. Made of the same pale earth, Old Laguna blends into its surroundings.

The frontage road is now marked New Mexico 124. Stay on it as it crosses a bridge over a deep arroyo. This arroyo is actually San Jose riverbed. In 1952, the wooden bridge that spanned the Rio San Jose caught fire when a petroleum truck crashed on it, igniting the structure and destroying it. This accident held up traffic on Route 66 for twelve hours. The *McKinley County Warrior* of Thursday, January 24, 1952 reported the event on the front page:

FLAMING TRUCK
BURNS 66 BRIDGE

A flaming crash that took the life of one unidentified man and seriously injured another stopped all traffic on Highway 66 from 8 p.m. last night until 8 a.m. this morning.

State police said the accident occurred at the bridge near Old Laguna Trading Post at around eight in the evening.

Cause of the accident was not known immediately but reports were that the fuel transport met another truck at the bridge. The transport plunged under the bridge and burst into flames that witnesses claim were some sixty feet in the air. The driver was pinned in the wreckage.

Equipment was being sent by the Highway Department from Albuquerque and Grants to make repairs on the bridge. Captain "Bob" Scoggins of the Gallup State Police Force said they were up all night routing traffic away from the blocked stretch on Highway 66.

What the newspaper account does not tell you is that when the bridge was destroyed, there was no way for the traffic on Route 66 to cross the San Jose. The Highway Department crews could not be assembled at the scene of the accident until late at night. They then had to build a detour from Route 66 to "older 66" so that the traffic could cross the Rio San Jose on an older bridge that spanned the riverbed. If you want to see the abutments of the old burned bridge look about 500 feet north as you cross the Rio San Jose.

It is hard for the present-day traveler, accustomed to concrete bridges and rapid-response disaster teams, to imagine any kind of accident that would hold up traffic on a freeway for twelve hours. Today there are always alternative routes, and other bridges. No one remains in a traffic slowdown for twelve hours. The old Route 66 travelers did not have such luxuries, if luxuries those are.

To visit the town of Old Laguna and its historic church, turn left at the gas station. Old Laguna is straight ahead of you.

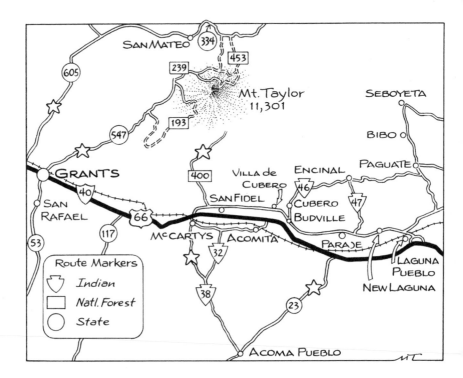

Map 3. Side Trips: Acoma, Mount Taylor.

OLD LAGUNA

TO GRANTS

OLD LAGUNA

The Laguna Indians are part of the band of Pueblo Indians who share the Keresan language. They have lived in this spot for hundreds of years. Their group was officially recognized by the King of Spain in 1689 when he graciously "gave" them the land that they had been occupying for generations. At the time, the King of Spain thought that this part of New Mexico belonged to the Spanish Crown. The King of Spain had never been to the New World and had never met a Laguna Indian. Nevertheless, he granted the Laguna people five square miles of land, which included a lake. The lake has long since dried up and turned into a meadow, but the description of the land and the lake persists. *Laguna* is the Spanish word for lake and the Laguna Indians called themselves *Pokwindiwe Onwi*, or the pueblo by the lake, long before the Spanish entered into their affairs.

In 1870, the United States Government involved itself in the thorny question of land ownership and Native Americans. It was decided that the King of Spain was correct and the Laguna Indians *did* have the right to occupy the land given to them by the Spanish Crown. The United States surveyor general made this determination official. One can't help but wonder what the Laguna people thought when the governments of the newcomers agreed that the Lagunas should live on the land they had always lived on.

Today the Pueblo of Laguna is among the most modern and progressive of all of the pueblos. Although some of the Laguna people are still living in the original pueblo that was built toward the close of the 1700s, many of them are living in the modern housing you can see scattered around the area. The Lagunas are reknowned for the programs and homes they have established for their elderly people and their comprehensive health programs for all the members of their group. The pueblo benefited financially from the uranium boom and has flourished under wise leadership.

"When 66 went by Laguna, times were different. There wasn't this big uranium boom. The Marmon family had the big trading post at Old Laguna and it was a real trading post, a place to buy groceries and hardware and necessities, not a tourist place. It was a big sandstone buliding with high ceilings, sort of dark and cool inside. It was right at the turn-off; you pulled off of 66 and by George, you were right in front of the place. I remember old man Marmon had this black mustache; it was heavy, very unusual at that time and of course a complete anomaly among the full-blooded Lagunas who were pretty much without facial hair. I heard that the Marmon brothers came to Laguna with the railroad in the 1880s. They worked for the Atchison, Topeka and Santa Fe. They married women from Laguna and became part of the community. One of the brothers is said to have been the civil engineer who designed the street system of Albuquerque. I bet there are a lot of drivers in Albuquerque who would love to get their hands on that man! I never knew if any of that was true; it's just talk I heard at one time or another. I always called on Marmon and was anxious to get on down the road. His place was never the beginning or the end of my day, just another call. Of course every call is a bonus if you're a peddler."

Laguna is also the hometown of Leslie Marmon-Silko, the award-winning author. Raised in Laguna and educated at the University of New Mexico, this lady draws on her personal experiences of living in two cultures to set before the perspective in her poems and stories. Her novel *Ceremony* is set in this part of New Mexico. Read this book and discover an entirely different history for the people and places along parts of old Route 66.

ENCINAL

After visting Old Laguna, turn back to Old 66 and head west. Just before you draw abreast of the Laguna-Acoma High School on the right side of the road, turn right on a dirt road that goes by the east side of the school. This is the road to Encinal or in the Spanish translation, "the oak grove." This is not an important stop on your trip down 66, just a pleasant ramble.

A short ways past the school, you will see some whitish hills or bluffs rising up on the right side of the road. If you are a picker-upper of rocks, but not necessarily a serious geologist, stop and climb among these white bluffs. One day as I was fooling around here, and the public address system at the school was giving the students instructions, I glanced down and found a bundle of long, slender stone needles, very similar to stalagmites or stalactites that are found in caves. I sat down in the dirt to examine my find. It was very puzzling to a nongeologist, as there was nothing close by that looked like a cave or a possible cave entrance. As I glanced around, I discovered another oddity. I seemed to be sitting in a field of stone turtles. Whether by fluke of nature or someone's hand, each of the hump-backed rocks near me had a smaller rock positioned close to it for a head and other smaller rocks situated to resemble feet. It was uncanny. Plants and weeds grew among the stones giving the appearance of naturalness but at the same time the distinct resemblance to turtles seemed unnatural. If you ever find this spot, let me know what you think. All explanations will be given serious consideration.

Back in your car, drive on to Encinal. Small and out-of-the-way as Encinal may seem, it has some interesting sights. One of the outstanding features of this hamlet is the rockwork. The bus shelter is made of native stone piled up into a welcoming, sheltering cup, and a stone water trough graces the center of the village. Nearby is a block of salt for livestock, something that is not often found in town squares anymore. Close to the square is a charming rock house whose ingenious builder also used unique and beautifully twisted cedar posts in its construction. The church in Encinal has lovely stained glass windows.

The time I visited Encinal, no was in sight but it certainly did not seem like a ghost town. As I returned to old 66, I spotted a cornfield about 100 by 400 feet, growing lush and green far away from the road. Encinal had all the signs of life.

PARAJE

Past the Acoma-Laguna High School, you will come to New Laguna, which is only a trading post/gas station/grocery-store. Going beyond New Laguna on old 66 will take you to Paraje, one of the Laguna villages. *Paraje* means "place" or "stopping place" in Spanish. Paraje is one the Laguna villages.

"When I was a young man, about twenty-five or so, I got the idea that I should quit my high life and get a job and make something of myself. This was the start of my career as a peddler. I got a position with the E. H. Krohn Company as a traveling salesman. Krohn was the distributor for Admiral appliances as well as a line of furniture and other stuff. I met the man whose place I was to take and he was supposed to take me around Albuquerque and up and down 66 and introduce me as his replacement. I didn't have much interest in this and he had even less so we decided to go down to the old Alvarado Hotel in Albuquerque and get drunk. We got there just before noon and had a drink or two and then he spotted a man he called Hugh Crooks. He introduced me to Crooks, who was a bachelor and ran the trading post at Paraje. Crooks spent the afternoon and evening with us and we drank and shot some pool and played some dice. Crooks told me to call him at Paraje and he would give me an order. I thought it was just drunken chit-chat but later on when I did call at Paraje, Hugh was friendly and we did a lot of business together.

One day I was at Paraje and Hugh pointed out one of his customers to me, a Laguna Indian, somewhat squarely built as many Laguna people are. Hugh told me that the man was blind and worked in the woodyard behind the store, cutting wood. It was difficult to believe but the next time I called at Paraje I went back to the woodyard and saw the man in action. He was truly blind but he had found his niche in the world as a woodcutter. He had a helper, a boy, maybe his son, who would pull the logs up onto the chopping block. When the log was in position, the boy told him so and he would go to work reducing the log to stove lengths. Each time he chopped through the log and made a length, he would stop; the boy would place the length on the woodpile and nudge the log up onto the chopping block again. At the signal that the log was in position, the woodcutter would go back to work.

I visited the woodcutter several times, oh, maybe five or six, and he was always calm and friendly. One time I took him a good file to sharpen his ax. He tried it out and I could see that he knew just how to use it whether or not he could see. I don't know if I ever met another man who was as suited to his work as the blind woodcutter of Paraje."

Before I-40 was built, when Route 66 was the main road, you had to turn off here and drive south if you wanted to visit the Pueblo of Acoma. You couldn't go to Acoma without driving through Paraje. The Paraje Trading Post was eventually purchased by the Cubero Trading Company and was operated by Hans Gottlieb for thirty years after Hugh

Crooks left the business. Today Hugh Crooks is dead and the Paraje Trading Post has been closed since 1987. Paraje is no longer the major stopping place on Route 66. Today, if you want to visit Acoma Pueblo, you don't have to travel through Paraje.

SIDE TRIP TO ACOMA

Leave Paraje, heading south on State Road 23. You are on you way to Acoma Pueblo or the Sky City of New Mexico. The people of Acoma are Keresan-speakers like their neighbors, the Laguna people. The town of Acoma is on top of a mesa about 350 feet above the desert floor. Tradition has it that the early Acomas established their town on the high mesa as a form of defensive protection. Not only was it difficult to scale the high cliffs of the mesa but also the people on the mesa top could see everything that moved for miles and miles in every direction. The view is beyond compare. Perhaps the beauty of the location was also valuable to the early Acomans.

Although the mesa's steep sides prevented the enemies of the Acoma people from surprising the mesa dwellers, the steep cliffs also presented a problem to the Acoma themselves. All the necessities of life had to be carried up to the mesa top. In the past there were two ways to gain the mesa top and visit Acoma. The "easy" way followed a steep crack up to the top of the cliffs. The "hard" way was a series of hand- and foot-holes carved into the side of a near vertical cliff. You can still see these hollows in the cliff. It is difficult to believe that people considered this a useful path. Did the Acomans simply learn where the hand-and foot-holes were when they were young, agile, and fearless? Did they become so used to this perilous path that it became a part of their everyday life and they never came to consider scaling a cliff as a risky experience?

Today a stone staircase of sorts is carved into the side of the cliff, and a rutty road that can accommodate cars also climbs to the top of Acoma. The people of Acoma prefer that you leave your car in the parking area at the foot of the mesa and walk the road up to their village. This is a good idea as you will find precious little space to park, drive or turn around in once you get to the top of the mesa.

There are tales of the early Acoma people resisting enemy invaders because they had such a strategic advantage on their high rocky perch. They couldn't be besieged because they had food supplies and a water source on the top of the mesa. They couldn't be overrun because they could pick any invaders off, one by one, as they scrambled up to the cliff top. This defensive system worked well until the Spanish came to the New World and declared ownership of all the land in the name of Spain. The Native Americans had never dealt with the Spanish and so were unaware that the Spanish were looking for gold, rich lands, and souls to save for Christianity, in roughly that order. Since the people of Acoma were not informed of this agenda, their relationships with the Spaniards quickly became as complex and rocky as the ascent to their town.

According to the research of Dr. Jack Forbes, scholar and historian, Juan de Oñate, a representative of the Spanish Crown, visited the pueblo in the fall of 1598 while searching for the bounty and riches of the New World. He asked for and was given a generous supply of food and blankets from the winter stores of the Acoma people. A month later, another part of Spaniards, following Oñate, stopped at Acoma and demanded more food and more blankets. This time the Acoma refused the request. It was December and they still had the rest of the winter before them. They would need their winter supplies themselves before warm weather arrived.

The Spaniards, angered by the refusal of the Acomas, sent eighteen men to the pueblo to take whatever they wanted, by force. All eighteen of the Spanish invaders were killed. In one historical account, eleven of the Spaniards perished on the mesa top and the remaining seven "escaped" the fury of the Acomas by jumping off the 360-foot mesa. Interpretations of history often depend on your point of view.

The Spanish viewed the actions of the Acoma people as insufferable. Oñate and his cohorts made plans to punish the people of the Sky City so severely that no member of the Native American population would ever defy the Spanish conquerors again. With this plan in mind, the Spanish road to Acoma and announced they wanted peace. The peace terms they offered, however, were designed to be so outrageous that the Acomans would refuse them and the Spanish could then massacre the people and say it was a defensive action against intractable savages. Under the terms of the peace treaty, the Acoma people were to turn themselves over to the Spaniards as slaves, see their town burned and leveled, and give all of their food and possessions to the Spanish as booty. When the Acoma refused, understandably enough, the Spanish soldiers responded by murdering 800 men, women, and children. The remaining Acoma people offered the Spanish food, blankets, and their valuables in exchange for being left alone, but the invaders refused and took captive 500 women and children and eighty men. They also took everything that the Acomans had offered them as tribute. Throughout this offensive, not a single Spanish life was lost.

After the battle, the Spanish meted out punishment for their captives. All of the female children over the age of twelve were turned over to Fray Alonso Martinez to be distributed across the Spanish Kingdom as the good father saw fit. All of the men over the age of twenty-five were to have one foot cut off and to be enslaved for twenty years. All of the remaining captives were also turned into slaves. It is to the Acomans' credit that most of them escaped from the Spanish, returned to their mesa top, rebuilt their town, and remained an anti-Spanish force for many years.

When news of the Acoma atrocity reached Spain, the king declined to discipline his soldiers in the New World. Morale there was said to be at a low ebb and the king did not want to add to the soldiers discouragement. He was afraid that the soldiers might give up on the New World and return to Spain. The Spanish Crown was hungry for the gold, land, and people of the New World.

Historical accounts like this bring to mind many questions. How many of the eighty men were over the age of twenty-five? How many of the girls were over twelve? How did the Spanish determine their ages? How could the girls be sent out of the immediate area? Who had the job of cutting off the feet of the captives? When this was done, did the victims bleed to death? What kind of first aid was available in 1599? Why do few of these details show up in the mandatory history of New Mexico class that all eighth graders in the state are required to attend?

Acoma is twelve miles from I-40. As you drive across the desert you will see several high white mesas in the distance. Which one is the mesa with the Sky City? It is impossible to tell at a distance. Make a bet with your traveling companions and gamble a bit as you drive along.

Along the road you will see a sign or two advertising the Acoma Visitors Center. Be sure to stop here before going on to Acoma. At the Visitors Center you can get information about any feast days or dances that might be going on at Acoma. In season you can catch a bus tour here that will not only will save you the problem of parking and hiking but will also be entertaining and informative. There is also a pleasant gift shop and a small museum that is well worth seeing. Once when I visited there, they were preparing an exhibit of old photographs. The pictures recorded one of the past governors of Acoma accepting an ebony-and-silver cane from a representative of Abraham Lincoln. The president was sending the gift to Acoma as a token of thanks for the honorable and peaceable conduct of the people of Acoma during the Civil War and the U.S. acquisition of the New Mexico Territory.

Another visit to the museum was highlighted by a new relic. The museum had just received the post office boxes and post office furnishings from the old post office at Cubero, New Mexico. Mrs. Roscoe Rice was the postmistress at Cubero for more than forty years. She was also the mother of Bud Rice, prominent citizen of nearby Budville.

The museum of Acoma is on a small scale but its holdings are unique and fascinating. They are also immediate. Displays in the museum are directly related to the people and countryside you have just driven through or the places you are about to see.

If you come to Acoma during the non-tourist season, it is still possible to tour the Sky City. Follow the signs to the foot of the mesa, park your car and walk up the road to the village. It is not a difficult or a long walk. At the top of the road you will see a house with a sign in the window announcing "Tours." This is the tour office of Acoma, and the people manning the desk can tell you when the next walking tour will depart. If it is a quiet day, the person on duty may take you on tour himself. There is a nominal fee for these tours and you must be escorted if you want to see Acoma. Just as you wouldn't want strangers wandering through your home unannounced or unescorted, neither do these people.

The tours of Acoma vary somewhat depending on your guide, but they all include the church as well as a walk through the narrow streets and a visit to the edge of the mesa. The church is immense, probably the closest thing to a European cathedral that could be contrived in 1625, considering the location and the materials available.

The best part of the Acoma tour is the people. When your tour begins, word goes out across the village. Soon ladies will be taking a seat outside their doorways next to small tables displaying pots or silver jewelry or other handcrafted items for sale. The tour guides are calm and relaxed and will stop the tour if you wish to look and talk and buy. The Acoma ladies are famous for their pottery, which has been declared some of the finest ceramic art in North America. When you stop by a doorway seller in Acoma you have the opportunity to buy both art and folk art. You may be speaking with someone famous like Lucy Lewis or you may be stopping by the home of a lady who likes to make a pot now and then to earn a little extra money for her household budget. You will also see some small works of art from the beginning potters. Little girls will be displaying their first attempts at pottery alongside the work of their mothers, sisters, and grandmothers. This is your chance to be a real patron of the arts. Buying a pot from the hands of a beginner can only encourage a little potter to keep on perfecting her craft.

THE CHICKEN PULL AT ACOMA

As a child, I used to accompany my mother as she drove various relatives out to Acoma on sightseeing tours. These trips were supposed to prove that New Mexico was a wild and romantic place or a dry and desperate land, depending on who the relatives were and how well my mother liked them. As we turned off of Route 66 and headed for Acoma, my mother would earnestly explain that the village we were about to visit was not the "real, old Acoma, but the *new* one, the one the Spanish came to in 1540." The old one, my mother would explain, waving vaguely at the other high mesas in the distance was "over there, completely inaccessible and yet more beautiful." None of us ever knew where my mother got this information. As far as I know, my mother never stepped out of her car between Route 66 and Acoma, yet she was able to convince numerous relatives about the beauty of "old Acoma."

One day in early spring my mother, my father, and I were trekking out to Acoma with my mother's brother-in-law and niece from Minnesota. My mother really liked these people and she was giving them the NEW MEXICO: LAND OF BEAUTY, COLOR, AND ROMANCE tour. New Mexico and particularly Acoma, did not let my relatives down. After we had arrived at the foot of the mesa and had climbed to the top, we were invited on a walking tour to see the village and the old church. When the tour was completed, the guide casually mentioned that if we cared to walk back down to the foot of the mesa and hike around to one side, there was going to be a chicken fight in a little while and we could watch. The chicken fight was going to be in honor of San Patricio. This sounded wild and barbaric to my uncle and cousin and they were eager to see it, but it seemed to make my mother a little hesitant. She had seen cockfights during her girlhood in Arizona and it wasn't what she wanted to show her in-laws. Was a chicken fight the same thing?

There were about a half dozen other tourists at Acoma that day and we all walked down the mesa and over to the spot the guide had told us about. There was nothing there. The morning grew hot and some of the less hardy visitors withdrew to their cars and drove off to places away from Acoma. There was no shade. There was nothing but New Mexican desert from Acoma to the horizon. We waited in the sun; we were accustomed to waiting with my mother. Everything was bright yellow hot.

Without warning, about twenty men on horseback whirled around the edge of the mesa and charged full speed to the spot where we were standing. The Indians were whooping and hollering, giving (may Jefferson Davis forgive them) the Rebel yell. This thundering horde came to a great sliding stop in front of the band of overawed tourists. The horses danced and pranced nervously. There were huge clouds of dust and jingling bridle bits and shouts and catcalls and words shouted in a language I couldn't understand.

I remember wondering about these men and horses, wondering why there was no one from Acoma waiting and watching with us. I wondered why these men on horses were dressed so simply in cowboy shirts and jeans; every other time I had visited an Indian Pueblo for a feast day or a dance, all of the Indians had been elaborately dressed in non-European clothes and all of them had been decorated with vast amounts of silver and turquoise jewelry. I remembered the time I had watched my grandfather chop the head off the old red rooster. I began to seriously doubt if I should be there in the hot Acoma sun, waiting for some unknown event called a chicken fight. If the Acoma people were not going to watch, should I be there?

Three of the men dismounted and others held their horses. I could see there were a few boys in the group but most of the riders were mature adults. Two of the dismounted men scooped out a small, deep hole in the sand while the third stood by, cradling a large black and white rooster. The rooster was placed in the hole, feet first, and buried with sand up to its neck. Only the neck, head, and bright floppy comb were left sticking up out of the desert floor. The three men remounted and once again the entire band of horsemen turned as a single unit and rode away in a wild charge into the desert. Once again they turned and charged back to the spot where the rooster was buried. Yelling and calling and slapping their saddle leather they raced each other back to the rooster.

When the turning, dusty crowd reached the buried bird, riding at top speed, elbowing each other for position, the rider in the lead leaned out of his saddle and pulled the buried rooster out of the ground. It was the most astounding piece of horsemanship I had ever seen in my young life and I was a regular fan of Roy Rogers, Gene Autry, and the Lone Ranger.

The man holding the rooster then reversed his grip on the bird from head to the feet, wheeled his horse around to face the oncoming horsemen and swung the rooster right into the chest of the first horseman he met. The Indians laughed and slapped their thighs; the tourists were simply speechless. This was not the picture of dignified Indians that they had expected. The riders elbowed each other and kicked their horses; they fought and rode and wrestled the rooster from each other. Every time a man gained control of the rooster, he began to flail away at his neighbor with it. The rooster began to loose blood and feathers. It became clear why the riders were not dressed in their best finery.

As the chicken fight went on, I could see that some of the men began to look for certain other riders to wallop with the rooster. It was if some of them shared a private joke, for the combat was carried on with high spirits and good nature. The riding band dissolved from the tight, twirling group it had started as and became a scattered crowd of tiring men and horses. A fat man on a black horse gained control of the bird and handed it to a boy on a buckskin horse. The boy was small, maybe seven years old, and slight. The rooster drooped from his two hands.

"Hit your Daddy! Hit your Daddy!" the fat man yelled. The boy paused; the reins were on the buckskin's neck. It took both of his hands and all of his strength to lift the rooster. He looked at the fat man and then at the man by his side, his father. The other men all shouted and whooped and watched the players in their midst. Decision made, the boy grinned, ducked his head and handed the bird to his father. The father rode like a dervish to the fat man and pounded him with the limp bird. The whole crowd, Indian and tourist alike, cheered him on.

When our little touristing group of relatives finally left the scene, the Acoma men were still whaling the tar out of each other with the dead rooster. I never saw another event equal to the men and horses at Acoma. I never saw such horsemanship again. In later years I did find out that what we had serendipitously witnessed was a chicken pull and not a chicken fight. I also found out that the people of Acoma watched it from grandstand seats on the top of their famous mesa while we tourists watched in the hot sun on the ground. My relatives from Minnesota never forgot their New Mexican vacation.

After visiting Acoma, you can return to the interstate the way you came in, or you can take a slightly more circuitous route north and west across the Acoma Reservation to the town of McCartys.

BUDVILLE

If you decide not to take the side trip to Acoma, stay on the road going past Paraje (New Mexico 124) and head west for a visit to Budville, Cubero, and San Fidel.

"This piece of road is old Route 66. It went right through those little towns, Budville, Cubero, and San Fidel. They don't look too impressive now, but in the days of Route 66, they were important places. Funny how a four-lane freeway can demolish little towns by just going around them.

Right where the road, old 66, begins to curve, just before you drive into Budville, there used to be an old rock house with a television antenna on it. That doesn't seem too unusual now and of course you can see satellite dishes all over the country today, but in the early fifties, a television antenna was a rarity. You could be driving along 66 and come to that house and people would be stopped on the side of the highway, taking pictures of that house with the antenna. They would have their Brownie cameras out, with big self-conscious grins, taking snapshots of that house. I guess they showed those pictures to their friends back home and talked about the modern developments that they had seen out West."

The town of Budville was established in the late 1920s. Roscoe Rice had a garage in the area and when Route 66 was built, his garage was right on the highway. Rice did a great deal of work on the cars that broke down on their travels between Grants and Albuquerque. Rice had a son everyone called "Bud" and in the late thirties Bud named the area Budville.

In the late forties, Bud expanded the garage to include a towing and wrecking service as well as a gas station and garage. Young Bud was an entrepreneur extraordinaire. He eventually became the justice of the peace for the area as well as the local vendor for brake and light stickers, license plates, and drivers' licenses. He operated a general store next to the gas station, which was also doubling as the Greyhound Bus stop.

Bud Rice's tow trucks were the only ones that operated between Rio Puerco and Grants. If your car broke down along that stretch of highway, you had to get Bud Rice to come and tow you in. He could fix

---

your car, too. If your car went off the road in bad weather, Bud Rice would come out of Budville and drag you back onto the highway. If the State Police stopped you for speeding, you had to appear before Bud Rice to pay your fine. And if your car was wrecked, Bud Rice would sell you a Greyhound Bus ticket so you could get out of Budville and be on your way. If Bud was busy, however, the broken-down motorist was not left on the side of Route 66. Mrs. Bud Rice, known as Flossie to her friends, would come to the rescue, driving one of the couple's big wreckers. Flossie not only drove the trucks and towed the cars, but she also functioned as a deputy sheriff. She went to the scene of auto accidents, made out reports, and represented the law.

"I remember the Rices of Budville. I used to call on them when I went up and down 66. They were good people, real hard working. And they always came out when you called. If it was two in the morning and your car was in the ditch and it was snowing, the Rices would come and pull you out. They were serious about their business. They were serious about what they did. I remember the first time I saw Flossie getting out of the wrecker. She was a little woman with a lot of black curly hair and fine eyes. If some man offered to do the work for her, fasten on the car, and tow it, she wouldn't let him. She did everything herself. She would hook the wrecker up to the car herself and pull it out of the ditch. 'Not bad for an ex-beautician!' she'd say. I guess she was a beautician before she met Bud Rice. She was a strong, capable woman.

I heard a lot of scandal about Bud Rice. People were always talking about him. I guess people always have a bad word for anyone who is successful. I always saw him as a businessman, working his tail off. He may not have been as pure as the driven snow; he had a rough tongue but he was no villain. He was murdered in a hold-up in 1967 or I bet he and Flossie would still be operating the wrecker service out of Budville. Flossie is still living there. She sold the wrecker in 1979 and she told me she was glad to close the doors of the garage. There'll never be another place like Budville again. There's no room for a one-man operation anymore. Everything has grown too big and that's a shame. There used to be a lot of hard-working men like Bud Rice, backed up by hard-working women. Making their own successes in the world. Independent. Tough. All gone."

Bud Rice and the wrecker may be gone but Rice left a unique legacy. He played a key role in the passage of a state law called the Anti-Bypass Law. Under this law, Interstate highways could not be built bypassing a community business area, unless the community consented. The law, which was intended to save small towns and businesses, had the effect of halting interstate construction in New Mexico for many years. Gallup was the last sizable town in New Mexico to consent to being bypassed. The next stop is Cubero. To get there, go past the gas station in Budville and turn right, taking the road that goes behind the Dixie Tavern. If you have driven past the tavern, you've gone too far and you'll have to turn back. This road is a loop off Route 66, known locally as "Older 66." This is the path the highway followed before it was rerouted in the thirties—bypassing Cubero.

CUBERO

Cubero is a short distance from Budville. Here you can see the old abandoned hotel and the building that once housed the Cubero Trading Post. The trading post is on your right as you come into town. It was actually a general store, and at one time you could buy anything from a refrigerator to a pack of gum here. Going inside was like walking into the past. It was dark and the ceilings were high. As you walked through the store, items from your early childhood and your parents' everyday world would catch your eye.

Cubero had a tumultuous past. In 1851 there was a plague of banditry around Cubero and the residents refused to accept gold in their business transactions because they feared robbery and murder.

The road west out of Cubero passes by some strange rock formations that seem to fashion a natural floor on either side of the road. When you cross a small bridge, you will see a creek cutting through a deep gorge that runs through the middle of Cubero. Follow this road to return to Route 66.

Cubero has been a bone of contention among New Mexican historians. It isn't known whether the town was named for the Spanish Governor Pedro Rodriguez Cubero, who was the Spanish Crown's representative in this area around 1700, or if it was named for a family of Cuberos who lived in the area when the town was built in the late 1880s. If you were to ask the old, regular travelers of Route 66 about the name of Cubero, those people might tell you it should have been named for the Gunn family. The Gunns had a cafe right where the road from the village of Cubero intersects with Route 66. This spot on the old highway is called Villa de Cubero. When Route 66 bypassed Cubero in the thirties, Sidney Gottlieb built a store, motel, and restaurant here to take advantage of the Route 66 traffic. In Villa de Cubero today, two of these buildings remain. One is a trading company called Cubero Trading Post and the other is a closed-up building called the Country Villa Cafe. The Country Villa Cafe is the site of the old Gunn's Cafe.

"I used to time my trips so that I would arrive in Cubero exactly at mealtime. There was a family there named Gunn who had a cafe right on Route 66 and the food there was well worth traveling for. The Gunns were excellent cooks and everything that came out of their kitchen was good. The Mexican food was superb. It was Mexican food, too, not this Tex-Mex stuff people cook up today. If you got to the Gunns at mealtime, and the Gunns knew you, they would invite you to have what they were having, not what was featured on the menu. 'We're having baked lamb today,' Mrs. Gunn would say, 'Do you want some?' And out would come a plate of baked lamb, steaming and tender with whatever vegetables were in season. You would sit there in that little cafe, eating this delicious food prepared with care and all fresh ingredients, and the traffic would go by on Route 66 and for a little while you could be happy and tranquil, feeling the way that genuine hospitality and good food make you feel. And then you would pay Mrs. Gunn $2 or $4 and go on down the road, satisfied."

You can still stop at the Gunn's Cafe. You can look through the windows and see the tables and chairs, quiet and dusty. There is nothing happening in the kitchen. No one is preparing roast pork or blue corn enchiladas. The travelers who come to Gunn's Cafe now remain hungry.

Just west of Villa de Cubero you will see O. B.'s Longbranch Saloon on the south side of the highway. The Longbranch Saloon is cool and dim inside as a proper saloon should be. In the summer it is a refuge from the long hot highway and the blazing sun. O. B. Hall, former Colorado native and expert heavy equipment operator, can be found behind the bar. Before O. B. became the proprietor of the Longbranch, he worked the heavy equipment at the Jackpile Mine. If you have time, and he has time, O. B. can tell you all about mining and working different mines in the West. Sometimes O. B. is helped out at the bar by his wife, Flossie. If you find yourself heading toward San Fidel out of Cubero, stop by the Longbranch for a cold one and a rest.

SAN FIDEL

San Fidel is just west of Villa de Cubero and the Longbranch. It's another small place on Route 66 and another problem to those people who want to know how towns are named and why. If you start reading over the shoulders of historians, you will find out two things about San Fidel: (1) San Fidel went through a number of name changes since it was settled in 1868, and (2) San Fidel was ultimately named for Saint Fidharleus or Saint Fidelis or Saint Faith. What these saints have to do with the town is something that I never discovered but I was always ready to put my money on Saint Fidharleus as the patron saint of the town because he sounded like someone's eccentric great uncle. You may choose to back one of the other saints, who are sure to be equally saintly and worthy.

Today there is not much to San Fidel. You can see some empty buildings and some crumbling ruins, but otherwise it looks like not much is going on in this quiet town. San Fidel is resting quietly on the edge of Route 66.

"There used to be much more to San Fidel. It was a place where you could dance and drink or eat and spend the night. See that crumbling building, just as you come into town from the east? The one that looks like it burned? On one side you can just make out a sign that advertises biscuits and gravy. That's where the Ramseys had their cafe on Route 66. Ramsey's place was as different from Gunn's as day is from night. Ramsey's was one of those places that started the notion that one should stop and eat where the truckers stopped because truckers knew where the best food was. I can remember coming through San Fidel and seeing six rigs pulled over, three on each side of the road and the drivers would all be inside, eating at Ramsey's.

The Ramseys served biscuits and gravy and mountains of fried potatoes and things like pies. When I remember San Fidel, I think of Ramsey's and food. I don't remember any special meals. I just remember food. Ramsey himself was a country-western musician. You could pick up any newspaper of the day and find an advertisement telling you that Ramsey and his band were playing in one of the clubs or bars or halls in Grants or Gallup or Top O' the World or any of those places along Route 66.

There was another thing I used to look for when I drove toward San Fidel. They had an airstrip near that town. It was a private airstrip, ran down the length of a cleared-out field, parallel to the highway. You could see the little hangar and a windsock billowing in the breeze. It was owned by Sidney Gottlieb, the man who built up Villa de Cubero. He was one of the first fliers in New Mexico, started flying way before I was traveling 66. His son Kurt was a pilot, too. He had one of those little old planes like a Piper or something and he kept it at the little strip. He must have had it for his own pleasure, it wasn't a business. He must have delighted in flying over all of the canyons and mountains around San Fidel. In a quiet place like that town, a plane must have been a real thrill.

Ramsey's Cafe still advertises biscuits and gravy.

I always liked San Fidel. I liked the country. Whenever I drove out of there heading west, I used to look to the north side of the highway, look up all of those little canyons running down from those steep and rocky mountains. I used to dream of building a home and I would try to pick out which canyon would be the best one. I wanted one that would be sheltered in winter but still open enough so that I could see the road and the countryside all around. I bet I never picked out the same canyon twice. I never built a home in San Fidel, either."

SIDE TRIP TO MOUNT TAYLOR

Leave San Fidel and drive west. About one-and-three-quarters of a mile from the town, you will find Forest Road 400 turning off to the north and snaking away, across the desert. If you are a wanderer and if you are camping out, this is a rewarding side trip. Forest Road 400 is a dirt road that heads toward the slopes of Mount Taylor. The adventurer starts out crossing the desert plain and eventually ends up in the tall ponderosa pines. Somewhere along this route you will find a

The perfect camping spot is a matter of taste.

cozy camping spot. If you are a wanderer and a picnicker, this is also a good trip for you. Pack your lunch basket and start out. The map describes Forest Road 400 as dirt. It is. It climbs into the tall pines and approximately eleven miles from 66, it meets Forest Road 501 at a microwave station. Forest Road 501 is for four-wheel drive vehicles. It is rough and rutted and rugged.

How far you go is up to you. When you get to your particular spot, stop and uncork a bottle of your favorite traveling wine. Savor the fine air. Your activities from here on out are your own business. If they do include bareskin activity, be sure and take some insect repellent, as you can encounter midges and other tiny biters in this area in certain seasons.

Mount Taylor is one of the four sacred mountains in the Navaho religion. In recent years there have been several plans proposed by various people who want to build ski resorts on the slopes of the 11,000-foot mountain. The Navahos have opposed these plans, arguing that such

Tall pines replace desert shrubs on the slopes of Mount Taylor.

a development would be a desecration of a holy place. Skiing on Mount Taylor would be similar to skiing in the Vatican. The problem is further complicated by the fact that the land does not belong to the Navahos or to the private developers. Mount Taylor is part of the Cibola National Forest. Under the existing National Forest philosophy, the land is held in stewardship for the use of all of the citizens of the United States. No one person or group can be favored over any other. So far, there are no ski resorts on the slopes of Mount Taylor.

When you are through with your frolic on the side trip to Mount Taylor, return to Route 66 the same way you came. Turn right onto the old highway and journey westward to Grants. Very soon, you will see the Whiting Brothers Motel on your right. Looking carefully, you can pick out a small sign that reads "El Rancho Jefe." or "the chief's ranch." In the heyday of Route 66, this used to be a tourist trap called the Chief's Rancho. It was built by E. J. "Chief" House, the founder and first chief of the New Mexico State Police. You can still see some signs, worn and faded now, that used to entice the motorist to stop and spend his money here.

"Those tourist traps were such a part of Route 66. It really wouldn't have been the same without them. Some of the businessmen would put up billboards along the highway advertising everything from bullwhips and moccasins to live rattlesnakes. And they carried everything they advertised. In a "good" tourist trap you could buy cactus in Mexican pottery planters, bullwhips and beaded Indian moccasins, Indian silver jewelry, lamps made out of cholla cactus, Indian pottery, cowboy hats and rubber tomahawks, soft drinks and those canvas waterbags that people used to hang on their rearview mirrors on the outside of their cars. You could find boxes and doodads made out of cedar and dolls dressed up like Indians—or the way people thought Indians ought to dress. And you could find Navaho rugs, all woven by hand, and steer horns. The array of stuff was dazzling. It was easy to spend your money if you weren't used to seeing that kind of thing. I think many people, many tourists would get caught up in the excitement of their trip and the idea of the Old West and Cowboys and Indians and would buy things they had no use for, and later had no desire for. What are you going to do with a bullwhip in Muncie, Indiana, for goodness sake?

Of course the operators of those places weren't selling quality and they weren't looking to do a repeat business with their customers. They just wanted to sell as much stuff as they could to each car that came along. I didn't do much business with those places, but I spent many an evening with the salesmen, the other peddlers, who did sell them those souvenirs.

I remember the Horn Man. His name escapes me right now but he was an older gentleman, even then; selling horns isn't exactly the career an eighteen-year-old would pursue. He had a car with a trailer behind and that trailer was filled with horns. You could see his outfit parked outside of any tourist anywhere up and down 66. He would be inside selling those mounted horns. He had horns with a ten-inch spread and horns that were sixty inches from tip to tip. All of them genuine steer horns. No fakes. He got them in Mexico, he said. Said the Mexican ranchers weren't like the American ranchers, who thought horns on a steer would cause him to lose fat. The Horn Man had a pretty wife, too. She was a Mexican lady and you would always see her sitting up straight and proud in the front seat of their car, waiting on the Horn Man. The Horn Man was dedicated, or maybe he just liked what he did. I saw him as late as 1975. His hair had gone white and he had a white beard but his clothes were pressed and his Stetson was sharply creased. He was parked outside of the Rio Puerco Trading Post. He was driving a station wagon and the back was filled with those horns and he was pulling a trailer. I couldn't tell about his wife, though. She didn't look much older than when I saw them in the fifties. If the Horn Man ever gives up his route, I guess people will just have to drive to Juarez to get horns."

If you wish to continue traveling on Route 66, the next stop will be McCarty's. Drive past the Whiting Brothers establishment, go over I-40 on the overpass and pick up 66 on the south side of the Interstate. Old 66 will parallel I-40 for a short distance here. If you look to your left you will be able to see the church at McCarty's, up against the hillside. Go under the railroad tracks, turn left, and go over a cattle-guard. A small sign that has "I-30" superimposed on an arrowhead will mark the road. Follow this road to McCarty's. There are other ways to get to McCarty's but this is the way 66 went.

McCARTY'S

If you have any interest in architecture or optical illusions and you have visited the church at Acoma, you should stop in McCarty's and look at the church there. It is easy to find, being the most prominent building in the village. This small church, snuggled up against the hillside, is an exact half-scale replica of the Acoma mission. After you've experienced the grandeur of the Acoma church and viewed the vast distance visible from the Acoma mesa, you may think this small church set in this small town seems to be a miniature rather than a full-scale building.

The plaque by the front door informs the visitor that the church was built in 1933 by the Marquette League of Catholic Missions to Indians. It is dedicated to the memory of Mary and Andrew White by their daughter, Mrs. Paul Talley. There is no explanation as to what connection Mary and Andrew and Mrs. Talley had to the people of McCarty's and this church.

This church served as a model for the University of New Mexico Alumni Chapel on the campus in Albuquerque because the McCarty's church was declared to be an "architecturally pure" example of Spanish Colonial architecture. In the interest of offending no one and favoring no religious groups, however, all the religious symbols were eliminated from the chapel built on the Albuquerque campus. The chapel was then acceptable for use by anyone of any religious persuasion.

Native American elements mix with traditional Catholic motifs in the church at McCarty's.

Enter the McCarty's church by the big front doors for maximum impact. If the big front doors are locked, try the side doors on the east. They are usually left open. The interior of the church is a blend of cultures and religions. There are signs here of both the traditional Catholic faith and traditional Native American belief, a characteristic typical of many Catholic churches built on reservations for dominantly Native American congregations. Ostensibly Roman Catholic, members of these churches also combine some elements of the indigenous religion with the symbols of Christianity. For example, one can occasionally find fine traces of cornmeal around the statues of the saints. Cornmeal, symbolizing pollen and life, is used as a blessing in Native American religious life. Instead of lighting a candle and saying a prayer to a favorite saint, one could say the prayer and sprinkle a bit of cornmeal. Instead of leaving a rosary at the foot of the statue of the Virgin, a member of one of these churches might leave a feather and a bead of turquoise. The extent of this cultural mingling is largely determined by the attitude of the parish priest. Some priests will tolerate and encourage a great deal of it, perhaps reasoning that religion must be a comfortable fit with daily life. Others will have no indigenous symbols in their churches, perhaps in an effort to make a clean and complete break between the worlds of the Native American religion and the sphere of the Catholic Church.

It is always interesting to visit churches like this one at McCarty's and see what balance has been struck between the two religions and the two cultures. The desire for beauty is almost always present, as is the feeling of human effort. The people decorating these churches seem to want to present the best of their lives and abilities in these places. Who could ever argue with a desire like that?

As you pull out of the church parking lot, turn left in order to head back to Route 66. When you reach the intersection with 66, turn left again onto it and you will be heading toward Grants. As you are driving along, you can see great banks of volcanic rock on either side of the road. This is the beginning of the lava flow or the *malpais*. There are more than 300,000 acres of lava flow here, under the supervision of the National Park Service. *Malpais* is the word made by putting two Spanish words together; *mal* or "bad" and *pais* or "country." Thus the traveler is entering the "badlands." In New Mexico, you may also hear the expression *malapie* (pronounced malla-pie) when someone is referring to the acres of lava flow. *Malapie* is formed by the Spanish word for bad and the corrupt pronunciation *pies*, the Spanish word for feet. *Pies* is pronounced pea-ays in Spanish but to an English speaker (and an English reader and writer as well) it looks like it should be pronounced pies, as in apple or lemon meringue. When all of this is put together you have acres of sharp-edged lava and there is no doubt that it is bad for the feet.

The Navaho do not have to be caught up in this debate over land that is bad or bad for the feet. To the Navaho, these lava flows have a different significance. According to the traditional stories, the Twin

War Gods were traveling this part of the country and making the world safe for people when they encountered a terrible monster. They slew the monster and its blood flowed out over the ground and hardened in the bright sunlight. The *malpais* is monster blood.

To the engineers of Route 66, the lava flow presented technical problems. The stone was very hard and difficult to work. It would be expensive to route the highway through the *malpais* so they planned Route 66 to go around the hardened lava. As you drive westward, you can see how the road avoids the lava outcrops. The old highway bridges are also placed away from the lava beds. By contrast, Interstate 40, which was built with a bigger budget and better technology, plows right across the sharp lava rock.

Stay on Route 66 as it travels on to Grants. You will have to drive through a tunnel to cross under Interstate 40. Turn left out of the tunnel and continue, driving Route 66. This road takes you behind Stuckey's at the freeway exit. It is marked Cibola County 16 but it is Route 66. Cross over the railroad tracks and spin into Grants, New Mexico.

GRANTS TO GALLUP

VIA ZUNI PUEBLO

GRANTS

Driving into Grants, New Mexico on Route 66 can be deceptive. The main road through town, which used to be Route 66, is named Santa Fe Avenue, after the Atchison, Topeka and Santa Fe Railroad. Traveling this street can give the wanderer the impression that Grants is a bleak and unlovely place. The closed stores and abandoned businesses seem to outnumber the flourishing shops and bright cheery cafes.

The key to Grants is to get off Santa Fe Avenue. Grants, unlike its first impression suggests, is a warm and welcoming place to visit. Once you turn off the main street, you will find tree-lined avenues, shopping centers, neat schoolyards, and modern buildings. The people of Grants are aware that their city does not impress at first glance, and as a result they are attempting to get the State of New Mexico to designate their main street as a historic section of Route 66. Once this official designation is established, the townspeople can improve Santa Fe Avenue. The Grants city council is already discussing plans to make Route 66 a showplace and a tourist attraction.

In the recent past, Grants was a uranium boom town. In 1950, Paddy Martinez discovered the first uranium ore near Grants at a spot called

---

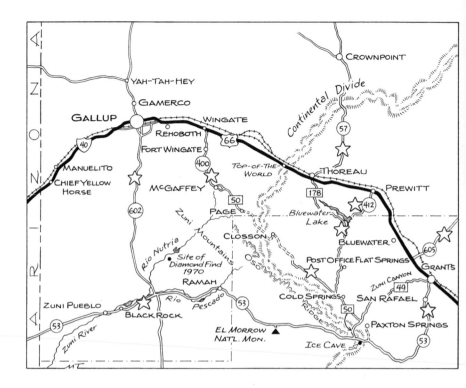

Map 4. *Grants to the Arizona Border (with side trips).*

Haystack Mountain, and from the fifties until the middle seventies, the town was the home of big-time mining operations. For more than two decades, you could count on finding a job in Grants. There was big business and big money to be made. The constant need for miners and construction workers, and for people to cook and care for them, and for ways and places for them to spend their uranium dollars made it a time of great prosperity. Every business along Santa Fe Avenue was open and thriving. There were new cars in the streets and people in the shops.

"I remember those times so well. Grants was a wide-open son-of-a-gun. Of course, I saw it from a different point of view than most people. I didn't live in Grants and I didn't work in Grants. I never visited the churches, never sent my kids to the schools, never had a neighbor in Grants. I didn't travel through Grants as a tourist, but I traveled through that town over and over; I knew that town. I knew the Sahara Club on the east side of town where there was always good honky-tonk music and fist fights. I knew the Grants Restaurant right on Route 66 where all of the construction men would gather for breakfast and dinner and tell tales of working and building deep under the ground. I knew the bars to visit on Friday nights where the men would flash wads of dollars from big paychecks. In the fifties, there weren't too many bars with television sets, but there were a few. There was one bar in Grants with a television and it was a big screen model. Every Friday night, that television would be tuned to a boxing program called 'The Friday Night Fights' and men would congregate there and bet on the fights. Oh, the money that changed hands on those nights! The proprietor of that bar, I don't remember his name, used to serve platters of spaghetti on Friday nights. Now that's a hell of a memory, isn't it? Isn't that historic? A bunch of men sitting in a bar, making bets and eating spaghetti? I don't know why we did that but we did it, over and over. It was a way of life."

Grants started out as a base camp for the men building the Atchison, Topeka and Santa Fe Railroad. It was sponsored by the railroad contractors John, Angus, and Lewis Grant, who established the camp in the late 1880s. Supplies would come into Grants' Station, as it was known then, and would be dispersed down the line to the men in the outlying camps who were building the railroad. These men were not only leveling the roadbed and laying the tracks, they were also cutting the timber and shaping the logs to the appropriate length for the railroad ties. The Grant brothers employed approximately 4,000 men to work on the railroad line, equal to slightly less than half of the current population. And those 4,000 men used 2,000 mules, a number one has to wonder about. Naturally, 2,000 mules were not kept all in one place. They would have been scattered out at the various camps for hauling and packing, as they were needed. However, if 2,000 mules could be lined up nose to tail, they would make a mule line that would reach almost three miles. That's a considerable quantity of mules, mule food, and mule by-products. From a business point of view, a person could lust for the opportunity to sell the Grant brothers the necessary 16,000 bales of hay a month that 2,000 mules could eat. There would be the problem of logistics and delivery, though. Who located the needed amount of food for the mules and then got it to the right places in the correct quantity at the appropriate time? There were no paved roads, no cars, no trucks. There were no personal computers to keep track of things. The Grant brothers might have lusted for a personal computer, if those had been available. The mules probably lusted for other mules, or horses, or donkeys. Mules are sterile but that has nothing to do with lust.

After the railroad was established, other types of industry came to Grants. In the early part of the century, lumbering and ranching were Grants' big businesses, and they flourished because the railroad could carry the cattle and timber to markets in other parts of the United States.

THE NEW MEXICO MUSEUM OF MINING

One of the notable attractions along old 66 in Grants today is the New Mexico Museum of Mining. Situated on the corner of Iron Street and Santa Fe Avenue, this modern, gleaming building also houses the Chamber of Commerce. You will be able to recognize the building by the high arched doorway and the huge pieces of mining equipment that sprawl across the green front lawn. At first glance these giant chunks of metal look like works of modern sculpture. They are enormous, and completely outside of most people's experience. But don't worry, after you visit the museum, you will know what those metal behemoths are and what they used to do.

The mining museum is exceptional on two counts. First, it is a success story. The museum started out sharing rooms with the Chamber of Commerce in an older building, a house on Santa Fe Avenue. At that time it was a people's museum in the sense that the artifacts were donated and curated by people living in and around Grants, and it contained a wonderful collection of objects from the lives of the railroaders, homesteaders, ranchers, and miners. There was also an assortment of Indian baskets and pottery as well as prehistoric remnants of early Indian life that had been collected by amateur archeologists.

Along with its presentation of historic objects, the old museum communicated an unvoiced message that seemed to say, "Times are changing. These items mark the past. Their owners and finders thought they were important enough to be in a museum. Look at them. Pay attention. There is something valuable here." It was up to each museum visitor to determine what was valuable and why.

In October 1986, the museum moved into the new building that shelters it today. Its operations have been bolstered by a large donation from the Taylor Foundation of Denver, a foundation named for Vernon Taylor, a man who lived in Grants and mined in the nearby Zuni Mountains during the 1930s. The New Mexico Museum of Mining now focuses on the mining industry that was so central to Grants for so long; it is sophisticated, well displayed, and beautifully appointed. And this brings us to the second reason you should take the time to visit the place.

The mining museum not only tells you about the history of mining uranium in Grants and the impact that had on the community, it also has a life-size replica of a working uranium mine on its lower level. People who were once uranium miners take museum visitors on guided tours to the lower level. Here you get the sensation that you have left the museum and are actually underground in a mine. The way that the tour guides touch the equipment and explain the daily life of mining tells the visitor more than any number of displays in glass cases ever could. There is a fee to visit the museum and the hours are listed on the front door. After a visit to the museum it is pleasant to walk across the street to Gunderson Park and watch the traffic roll down Route 66. Gunderson was a long-time resident, businessman, and interested citizen of Grants.

THE MOTHER WHITESIDE MEMORIAL LIBRARY

Around the corner from the mining museum is the Mother Whiteside Memorial Library. This modest library is a monument to a woman who made a difference. In the twenties, thirties, and forties, Mrs. Whiteside ran a boardinghouse in Grants. Many of her boarders, who were frequently single men living far from their hometowns and families, worked in the mines or for the railroad. Mrs. Whiteside created a home for them, serving family style meals and looking after the people living in her establishment. She nursed the men when they were sick or injured and took a lively interest in them. She was also involved in her community. When there were no doctors available, Mrs. Whiteside served the Grants community as a midwife. (At the time of this writing, there were seven doctors in the Grants area and about half that number of veterinarians.) When Mother Whiteside passed away, Vernon Taylor, who had lived at Mother Whiteside's boardinghouse before his rise to mining executive, contributed money to establish a town library as a memorial for his friend and landlady. The railroaders also collected funds and the library was built. Everyone hoped that Mother Whiteside would approve. She had improved their lives and they passed that on to their town in the form of the first library for Grants.

SIDE TRIP TO LA MOSCA LOOKOUT

If you grow tired of history, people, and places and are ready for a wander in the San Mateo Mountains, take State Highway 547 northeast out of Grants. This road is also called the Lobo Canyon Road. Before you leave Grants completely, though, stop in at the District Ranger Station on Lobo Canyon Road and pick up a map and check the road conditions.

This side trip will take you along State Road 547 to the Lobo Canyon Campground, on a rough road tour of a picturesque loop of Forest Road 193, through the high country, and back to State Road 547. Then you have a choice of traveling on to visit the La Mosca Fire Lookout or returning to Grants. Whether you decide to make this an afternoon picnic or an overnight camping adventure, you will be seeing some beautiful, tranquil country. You will be able to view wildflowers in season, wild birds, and very few homo sapiens. Unlike the desert, this country will not impress you with the struggle of living in a hostile environment and wide sweeping spaces. The San Mateo Mountains will show you a panorama of tall trees, tall mountains, and natural majesty.

About five miles out of Grants on State Road 547, look to your left and see a high, chalk-white wall surmounted by a crag of heavily scored rock. This is what remains of the Pumice Corporation of America's mine. The company worked this area in the 1930s and 1940s. You are in the vicinity of private land completely surrounded by U.S. Forest land. Most of the private land is dotted with mines and mining operations, some working, some defunct. Pull off the road and get out your camera. Geographic features like this bring out the Ansel Adams in every camera-toting wanderer.

Eight miles from Grants turn right onto Forest Road 193. The Forest Service sign will tell you that this is the road to Lobo Canyon Campground. The road is dirt here and its condition will depend on the season and the time passed since it was last graded. It is usually passable in most passenger cars. The road will wind past the concrete picnic tables and restrooms of the picnic ground. It soon grows narrower and changes from a dirt road with three distinct ruts to a dirt road with two ruts. This is not a road you want to travel quickly. Take time.

The road will begin to climb and you will notice that the vegetation begins to change. Coming out of Grants, the trees at roadside are small and shrubby, mostly piñons and cedars. With the slight change in altitude, the piñons give way to the taller, straighter ponderosa pines. Ponderosa pines are trees of the mountains. Although they can be found as low as 4,000 feet, (and lower, if they have a source of water), they flourish between 6,500 and 9,000 feet. They are good marker vegetation to help you gauge the elevation.

Ponderosas have thick, interesting bark that looks remarkably like a jigsaw puzzle. You can start to take it apart, with the idea of reassembling it like a picture puzzle, but you will eventually discover that the pieces do not fit together like the typical, two-dimensional puzzles. Ponderosa pine bark does have the "ears" and "notches" of a puzzle but it is three-dimensional instead of two and the pieces interlock across all three of the dimensions. I have never been able to reassemble a ponderosa puzzle, no matter how carefully I picked it apart and how systematically I spread out the pieces of bark. Handling the stuff makes your fingers smell nice, though.

That is another distinctive characteristic of the ponderosa pine. It has a delightful aroma of vanilla. On a warm day, if you step up to a ponderosa and take a good whiff, you can smell this delicious scent. This would be a good time to indulge in a bit of tree hugging, if you care for that sort of thing. If you are going to embrace a tree, it may as well be one with a wonderful smell.

The drive from the Lobo Canyon Campground back to State Road 547 via Forest Road 193 is about eleven miles. Somewhere along those miles you will find the enchanted glade, on the side of the road, the sheltered spot, out of the wind. Stop here and get out of your car. Walk among the trees and flowers. Try to hear the sound that silence makes. It is rather like a high-pitched whine. You usually can't hear it if the wind is blowing and some people never hear it because it is such a high frequency. It is pleasurable, though, to get yourself quiet and see if you can identify each of the forest sounds until the only sound left unlabeled is the sound that silence makes. Once you hear it, you will be able to pick it out easily, ever after.

When you re-encounter State Road 547, you have a choice. You can turn left and journey back to Grants or you can turn right and go on to the La Mosca Lookout. To reach the La Mosca Lookout go a bit more than three miles along State Road 547 and turn right onto Forest Road 453. Follow the signs to the lookout. If it is early spring or summer, and the tower is open, the lookout may allow you to climb up and survey the land from the high perch. If it is fire season, the lookout may be too busy to welcome visitors.

Return to Grants via New Mexico State Road 547 south and west. As you drive along, you should be able to see Mount Taylor on the left. Its blue cone reaches 11,301 feet toward the sky.

A SOUTHERN ROUTE TO GALLUP

If your business or your conscience isn't demanding that you barrel down Route 66 and reach Gallup quickly, then consider taking the southern route to that city. This trip, which goes via New Mexico State 53 and 602, won't reveal anything about Route 66 but it will take you to some of the less well-known historic spots in New Mexico. You will also get to see some more of New Mexico's varied and dramatic landscape.

Turn south off Santa Fe Avenue where the signs indicate access to I-40. Go over the interstate and head south on State Road 53. As you drive along, you will begin to see chest-high rock banks on the right side of the road. They are clearly marked with horizontal layers of various materials laid down thousands of years ago in a different geological age. The rocks are also clearly marked with vertical scoring every eighteen inches or so. The vertical lines are the remains of deep holes made in the rock when the road was under construction. At regular intervals workers drilled a shaft and packed it with explosives. The explosives were set off and the rock banks were blown to kingdom come. After the debris was cleared away, the road was built on the now flatter ground. It seems a great deal of effort to achieve a smooth grade. Hilly roads can be more entertaining but that is probably not a consideration of highway engineers. About two miles outside of Grants the road forks and a small strip of highway heads to the right. Take this road for a short detour through the village of San Rafael.

SAN RAFAEL

San Rafael is a small pleasure to see. The one long street is tree-lined. As you drive along you will see that everything in San Rafael is carefully lined up along this single short street. The Palomas Bar is first, then come the church and the bell tower. The crucifix from the churchyard stands sentinel right on the edge of the street, giving the idea of how narrow this road must have once been. As you go toward the end of the village, you pass houses of many descriptions, all sheltered among large, leafy trees. Some of the buildings in San Rafael were built in the late 1860s when Fort Wingate was headquartered in this area. These buildings are to the east of the main street and are considered to be fine examples of New Mexico Territorial architecture. Finally you reach an old-fashioned traffic signal that marks the end of the village. You can pass through this tiny community so quickly that you can miss its oasis-like charm. Before you know it, you are through and the road begins to carry you back to the highway. In the summertime, passing through San Rafael is like a single breath of cool, green air.

In any season there is one more attraction in San Rafael. At the west end of the village, near its boundary fence fronting the road, there is a large barn and stable yard. Living in this barn and sauntering around the yard are great, majestic Percheron draft horses. These are not the wiry and intelligent cutting horses so typical of the Southwest. These are not the elegant Arabians or the quick Quarterhorses. These are the powerful draft horses of legend, whose ancestors came from the Perche region of France. These horses are on a scale slightly larger than life, mighty, yet quiet and calm, easy in their strength. Their muscles don't ripple but you have the sense that under the sleek horsehide is more muscle, bigger muscle, and more potential than most horses have. In the earlier days, horses like these were essential to the lumbering industry of Grants. In spite of the convenience of the railroad to take the timber to market, men and horses still had to walk into the forests, cut the trees, and snake the logs out of the hills. The Percherons were the horses of choice for this task.

Back on State Road 53, you will be crossing wide meadows bordered by ranks of piñons and ponderosa pines. In the 1850s this land was cultivated by the United States Army, which maintained hay fields for the livestock at Fort Wingate. Fort Wingate was first located in Seboyeta in 1850 and later moved three miles south of Grants, just east of San Rafael. This is where Kit Carson was stationed when he began his famous (or infamous, depending on your viewpoint) efforts to round up all of the wily Navaho and incarcerate them.

In the late fall, this landscape is filled with color. The green and gold wildflowers spring out of the red earth and compete with the blue sky and the white clouds for your attention. The grey-black highway shoots across this riot of color. The air is clean and intoxicating. You are the first person to breath it. This is the time of year to cross New Mexico on a motorcycle and experience the color and the air in an immediate way. A motorcyclist would have no regrets on this trip unless it rained. When New Mexico is dressed up in color, one can forget poet Don Blanding's description of the "land of cruel beauty."

Twenty-six miles from Grants you will see a sign directing you to turn off the highway and visit the ice caves. This will not be the first billboard you have seen touting the ice caves, and if you are ready for a bit of commercialism, the ice caves are ready for you.

THE ICE CAVES

The ice caves are a genuine, natural, and unusual phenomenon. Cool air flowing out of deep, underground chambers sweeps across small amounts of water that have seeped out of the lava beds of the malapais. The constant flow of cool air freezes the tiny water holes. As new moisture collects, it is frozen on top of the existing ice. After many years of this, the ice build-up is extensive and remains through all of the seasons.

The ice caves outside of Grants are a private venture owned by David and Reddy Candelaria. When the Malpais National Monument was established, there was some discussion about the National Park Service acquiring this interesting spot and converting it to a Visitor Information Center. At the time of this writing, however, the Candelarias were still promoting their natural wonder as they have for more than forty years. When you arrive at this establishment among the pines, you will see a roomy parking lot, a collection of buggies, wagons and old ranching equipment displayed in a fenced enclosure, and an information-gift shop in a rambling, rustic ranch house. This spot in New Mexico is lovely. The trees are tall and the breeze sighs among them.

After you pay your entrance fee, you are free to walk at your own pace to the ice caves. The walk is short, along a broad, well-maintained trail. Most of the trail is very flat, smooth, and wide. As you stroll along (this is by no means hiking), you will be walking right through a spill of ancient lava. You can see firsthand how sharp and brittle the lava is. Wildflowers and bushes have taken root in the cracks of the lava and present many photo opportunities. There is no litter and everything is very pleasant. The walk itself could be worth the price of admission.

At the end of the trail, you will find a long flight of broad, sturdy wooden steps. At the base is a viewing platform that gives you an opportunity to peer into the back of a small natural amphitheater made of hardened lava. In the back of this curving space is a wide swath of gritty grey-green ice. You can feel the cold air blowing across the ice. The sign on the platform railing warns you to remain on the viewing stage and not to venture out onto the ice. If you had become hopelessly lost in the *malpais* and were making your way through the heat and blinding sun, dodging rattlesnakes and cactus, it would be an unimaginable delight to find one of these natural ice formations.

The walk back to your car follows the same enjoyable path. On the return trip, however, the hard part of the walk is the climb up the wooden staircase. Retrace your steps and return to your car. Drive back to Highway 53, turn left, and head west.

SIDE TRIP TO OSO RIDGE LOOKOUT

A short distance west of the ice caves turnoff on New Mexico 53 you will find Forest Road 50. Turn right here if you wish to visit the Oso Ridge Lookout. In two miles you will find Forest Road 187. Turn left, and the lookout is one mile farther on.

As you drive deeper and deeper into the forest you leave the piñon and juniper and ascend into the ponderosa pine belt. The smell of pine and vanilla is heavy in the air. If it is late summer or early fall, there will be tall spears of mullein on either side of the narrow road. The tall lances of the mullein arise from a basal rosette of velvety, downy leaves. The tall stalks have heavy heads of yellow flowers. The mullein plant is an infinitely useful herb. Its large soft leaves can be used as toilet paper or they can be sewn into a sleeping cap to help relieve a face ache. The yellow flowers can be steeped in sweet almond oil and used to remedy an ear ache. Even if you are not an advocate of herbal concoctions, mulleins are a pleasing sight.

The last half-mile to the lookout is the worst. You may wish to walk it but by the time you decide on that you will be faced with the problem of abandoning your car in the middle of the road. There is no place to park and absolutely nowhere to turn around. Once started, you will have to creep on or back all the way down the hill. A wanderer's life is full of tough decisions.

The Oso Ridge Lookout is perched on a narrow ridge where U.S. Forest land and private land meet. The lookout tower is right smack on the boundary. Besides the tower itself, you will find several small outbuildings scattered over the very small area that comprises the top of the ridge. The buildings are not the main point of this excursion; the reason for struggling to the top of Oso Ridge is the view. From this vantage point you can see a vast sweep of New Mexico, with a sampling of many of the different types of land that make up the state. To the southwest and east, the *malpais* is spread before you with its sharp rocks and severe silhouettes. To the south you can see the Zuni Mountains descending from the high pines and dwindling away to the desert. Westward the Zuni Mountains and Oso Ridge march into the distance, enveloped in pines, or as Robert Service once described, "pines and pines and shadows of pines."

If you visit Oso Ridge during the fire season, which is May through July, you may be invited to climb into the tower for an even more splendid view. At the time of this writing, the tower was being staffed by Buck and Ruby Keeney, who work as private contractors for the U.S. Forest Service, watching for wildfires. From May to July, these two vital, lively retirees maintain a nine-hour-a-day, seven-day-a-week watch. If they spot smoke or fire from their perch on the high ridge, they radio its location to the dispatcher in Albuquerque. From Albuquerque, information is passed on to the ranger station in Grants and fire-fighting crews and equipment are organized from the Grants location.

When not working in the tower, Buck and Ruby live in a secluded house not far from Oso Ridge. Accompanied by their pets and grandchildren, they seem to enjoy life in the forest. Among their pets are some frolicsome Nubian goats with floppy ears and almost human-sounding voices. When you see Ruby chasing a mischievous billy through the trees, it's easy to forget that you are watching a grandmother. Three months out of the year, the Keeneys are snowbound; their only access to the outside world is a snowmobile. Buck and Ruby don't seem to mind the isolation; in fact, they seem to relish it. The same way to escape from the humdrum that motivates the wanderer is something that these people have incorporated into their daily lives.

Ooze carefully down the hill and take Forest Road 187 back to Forest Road 50. At the junction of these two roads you have three options: (1) You may return to New Mexico State Road 53 and journey onto Gallup (2) You can take a side trip to Rivera Canyon and search for a lost relic of the past (3) You can return to Grants via the scenic trip through Zuni Canyon.

THE ZUNI CANYON RETURN

If you select the option to go back to Grants, turn left onto Forest Road 50 and follow it until you find the classic fork in the road. (This is not just a classic fork in the road, it's a big, unmistakable one, complete with road signs.) The left-hand fork will continue as Forest Road 50, while the right-hand fork, which you will follow, is Forest Road 49.

This route to Grants is simply nice. After several hours of creeping up narrow trails and over rutted dirt roads, Forest Road 49 is soothing. It is wide and smooth, even if it is dirt. This is a tranquil drive of about fifteen miles to Grants, and during this time you see some lovely, gentle scenery. A single-lane bridge spans Agua Fria Creek. The red hills alternate with white hills in an easy counterpoint. The bald side of Mount Taylor presents itself in stately splendor.

Zuni Canyon is a comfortably close canyon: not too wide as to be intimidating, not too close as to be suffocating. This canyon is just right. All too quickly you will come to the outskirts of Grants. The Forest Road will give way to the city street. Welcome back to Grants, New Mexico.

SIDE-SIDE TRIP TO RIVERA CANYON

The side trip that is about to be described is not really a wild goose chase. Think of it as an extended exploration with an unfinished ending. At the junction of Forest Road 187 and Forest Road 50, turn left onto 50 and travel until the road splits. Forest Road 50 goes off to the left and Forest Road 49 heads right. Stay on Forest Road 50. About two miles on, you will find another dirt road branching to your left and going *through* Rivera Canyon. Turn here. This road will go about two miles and will meet Forest Road 187 again. Rivera Canyon, however, is your destination.

Around the turn of the century, there was an extensive lumbering operation in the Zuni Mountains. Not only did men and horses cut and drag timber down from the slopes of the mountains, but a vast network of narrow-gauge trains traveled through the mountains collecting the timber harvest and carrying it to the railhead at Grants. Charles O. (Chalky) Breece was the man responsible for developing the rail system in Zuni Canyon.

For the most part, the little trains were pulled by Shay engines. Contradictory references from reliable sources say these little steam engines burned either green wood or coal. They took on fuel and water at Paxton Springs, about six miles north of the ice caves (the same area where Mike Todd, husband of Elizabeth Taylor, lost his life in a plane crash). The little trains chugged all over the Zuni Mountains. It was often more expedient for them to cross a deep canyon on a trestle than to chug down one side and up the other. These railroad trestles were built of wood and were manmade fashioned with very little machine power. There is one still standing in Rivera Canyon, somewhat hidden by brush, trees, vegetation that has grown up since it went out of use.

I have never seen this wooden, handmade trestle. I don't know where to tell you to look in Rivera Canyon if you want to see it. I have heard many conflicting stories about it. I hope you find it if you start out to look for it. It would be so magnificent to find this relic of the past, shrouded in bushes and still waiting for a narrow-gauge timber train to come steaming along, loaded with logs. You may never get to the deep and dark jungles to search for the hidden and mysterious civilization of Zog, but finding the old wooden trestle in Rivera Canyon might be a satisfactory, substitute thrill. Do you want to start hiking?

Write if you find it; take a picture if possible. Write me a letter about your adventure and send it to this publisher.

A last note: if you go off into the forest for an explore, remember to take jackets, matches, a canteen, a compass, a map, and a companion so that you will not get cold, lost, hurt, scared, lonely, or all of the above. The ranks of bonafide wanderers are thin enough without losing anyone to disaster.

ON TO GALLUP BY NEW MEXICO 53

Backtrack to New Mexico State Road 53, turn right, and head west. You are once again on the road to Gallup. As you proceed to the west, Oso Ridge will be slanting away to the north and west. It runs on for 60 miles, forming a high spine through the Zuni Mountains.

Most of the attractions in this part of New Mexico have been of the scenic and historic variety. Some very fine artists live in this part of the state, however. Oso Ridge is the home of Amy Adshead, intaglio artist and lithographer. Amy Adshead is a recognized talent in New Mexico and the art world beyond the state boundaries. Like all masters, Amy Adshead can make the difficult, the complex, seem easy, understandable, and joyful.

I first met Amy Adshead at an arts-and-crafts fair. She was displaying her work and I was intrigued because the subject was Coyote. (This was years before the Coyote Craze of the late eighties.) In the midst of all of the potters, jewelers, watercolor artists, and solemn art patrons, Coyote was making an appearance. Sly trickster Coyote, the Wild Dog that brought fire to humanity, was at an arts and crafts fair. Coyote was doing his best for Amy Adshead or perhaps, Amy Adshead was doing her best for old Coyote: bargains and partnerships with Coyote rarely turn out as one might expect.

Amy Adshead had portrayed Coyote and the Stars. At the Beginning, when stars were new, Coyote grew tired of listening to the discussion of how the stars should be placed in the sky. In typical Coyote impatience, he grabbed all of the stars and threw them, helter-skelter into the night sky. That is why the stars are not neatly fixed in careful geometric patterns today. Coyote is not a patient character; Amy Adshead is. In a small space, smaller than six inches square, Amy Adshead had put Coyote and the Stars. It was amazing.

In the following years, Amy Adshead turned up at most of the arts-and-crafts fairs I attended. She usually had Coyote to display with her other subjects. And her other subjects were always interesting, delicate, thoughtful. She invented new, small countries and designed buildings, postage stamps, and languages for them. She portrayed scenes and animals from her life on Oso Ridge. Amy Adshead became well known and her work began to appear in serious art galleries. Although the galleries were serious and big time, Amy Adshead continued to make images that were skillful and artistic and at the same time, the images laughed quietly and tugged at the mind with a mischievous grin. When Amy Adshead is not involved with lithography, she designs and creates environmental settings for zoos and museums.

New Mexico 53 now shoots across the landscape of flat clearings edged with stands of ponderosa pines. Among the trees you will be able to spot an occasional cabin or ranch house. Near one of these dwellings is a sign advertising hand-carved tables. If you are a woodworker or an aficionado of the handmade, this is an interesting stop on your journey.

Again, the land begins to flatten out. The vista becomes wider and the edges of the land move away from the highway. High bluffs rise up in the distance. Numerous signs advertising land for sale flash by and tempt the wanderer to give up and settle down. Clouds decorate the rimrock on the bluffs.

New Mexico clouds aren't like other clouds. They have a wider, more dramatic stage to appear on than other clouds do. New Mexico clouds take advantage of this. Clouds in New Mexico always seem to be a bit larger than standard. Given all of that extra sky, clouds in this land seem to stretch out and be more than clouds. The traveler rarely sees sweet little bits of fluff frisking across the sky. Instead the traveler is given huge clouds, towering thunderheads, giant masses of cloud stuff. Clouds in New Mexico are often so exaggerated that they look artificial. The cloud watcher sees an overwhelmingly dramatic set of clouds and thinks, "That's outstanding. That's beautiful. Some painter should paint a picture of those clouds." Then after a moment of thought, the cloud watcher realizes that if there were a painting of those clouds, he or she would take one glance and immediately think: "No clouds look like that. That artist imagined those clouds. Who would buy a painting of fake clouds?"

Clouds in New Mexico don't come in simple regulation colors like black, grey, and white. Clouds in New Mexico can be red, purple, yellow, blue, and green. They get edges and linings of gold and silver. They pose in front of red cliffs, green trees or lavender mountains and dazzle the observer. If observers were not seeing the cloud show with their own eyes, they would not believe that the theatrical display was real.

It is difficult to talk about these extraordinary clouds with another person. It is difficult to find someone who will understand when you say, "Hey, I saw this beautiful cloud. It was pink and gold and had red and purple streamers and the sun was going down so after awhile the entire sky turned blood red and the sunlight streamed like liquid gold through some small openings in the cloud and it looked like an Italian Renaissance painting. Then the sky turned grey around the clouds and it was breathtaking." These are not easy conversations. After all, the subject is just, well, *clouds*. Sometimes it is easier to say, "The clouds at sunset were nice tonight." And everyone in hearing distance will say, "Yeah they were, very pretty." New Mexicans don't want to talk their clouds to death.

EL MORRO

Thirty-seven miles from Grants, more or less, you come to El Morro National Monument. What you will see is a great chunk of cream-colored rock with some scrubby growth at its feet, rising out of the flat desert floor. This monolith is very large and hard to miss. It is the type of important landmark that travelers and wanderers note and say, "Today we'll go in the direction of that big bluff and if we make good time, we'll camp there tonight."

A great many travelers and wanderers have made it to the side of this desert crag, and what they found when they arrived was a delightful camping spot. There was a small spring and the high walls cast tall, cool shadows providing relief from the desert sun. These walls were once smooth sandstone. The sandstone was soft enough to mark or draw upon using pointed sticks, rocks, knives, or swordpoints. Many visitors to El Morro did write or draw upon the rock. Whatever there is about blank walls that compels the human animal to leave his mark was present at El Morro.

Early Native Americans left pictographs scratched into the stone. Spanish conquistadors left names, dates, and complete sentences explaining who they were and why they were journeying in that part of the world. Later, settlers, cowboys and tourists all left their own messages on the rock. Though the Spaniards named the place El Morro, which translates simply into "bluff" or "fortress" (the bluff does look like a fortress in the desert), the English-speaking population began to call the spot Inscription Rock.

The earliest dated message carved into the sandstone was left by the Spaniards in 1605. The redoubtable Juan de Oñate came by El Morro on April 16, 1605 on his way back from an exploratory venture to the Gulf of California. He carved or had carved this information into the sandstone at El Morro. The inscription and the information it conveys is interesting but it provokes many questions. In 1605 El Morro was an isolated landmark in a remote spot in the very recently explored New World. Few people lived in this part of the world and even fewer of them could read or write Spanish. Why, then, did the Spaniards carve their names and dates of passage into the rock? Did they expect someone to travel by and read it? Was it proof of the Spanish conquest of the New World? Was it simply graffiti, a Spanish version of "Kilroy was here"? Or was there a more ominous reason for writing on the rock? Was life and travel so perilous in the New World that this message was left in case the Oñate party met with disaster? Was it put on the rock as indicator in case they did not return? The wanderer will have to journey to El Morro and look for the answers to these questions himself.

In 1906, three centuries and a year after Oñate passed through, President Theodore Roosevelt signed the legislation that made El Morro a national monument. In 1933, it became part of the National Park System. By this time the inscriptions on the monument had been counted and catalogued. There were over 500 separate "messages" on the rock.

The people in charge of preserving this historical site had a problem. They could and did build paths and trails so that visitors to El Morro could tour the site and see the many inscriptions. They could prevent the tourists from defacing the monument and adding new inscription to the sandstone. They could not, however, stop the wind. Year by year the blowing wind, carrying tiny sand particles, was polishing the carvings off the face of El Morro. It was not feasible to put the entire butte behind protective glass. The oldest inscriptions were finally covered by a transparent panel, but the rest remain exposed. They pose a problem in preservation and another puzzle at El Morro.

Today, the traveler may visit El Morro and see the inscriptions. There are well-marked paths, nature trails, and information about the ecology of the sandstone cliff. There are picnic tables and camping sites and for those with the creative urge, a special piece of sandstone has been put aside to accommodate the inscribers of the twentieth century.

RAMAH

After leaving El Morro, turn left and head west on State Road 53. The blacktop carries you across more wide landscapes. To the right or the north, striped rock formations abutt a white cliff. Wide fields stretch away on either side of the highway. These fields are bounded by neat strands of barbed wire. Blue-notched cliffs covered with evergreens begin to appear in the distance. The air is clean and clear. The striped rock formations begin to take on a definite red-and-white pattern. Soon you will spot the sign indicating the turn-off to the Ramah Navaho Chapter House.

The Ramah Navaho are a small band of Native Americans indigenous to this Area. They did not name themselves the Ramah Navaho. Ramah is a small farming community up the road. The Navahos were living here before the town of Ramah was established. Like the Cañoncito and Alamo Navahos, the Ramah Navahos have a reservation that is separate from the big Navaho reservtion that straddles the New Mexico-Arizona border.

Right after the Ramah Chapter House turnoff, you will come to the Lewis Trading Post. This huge metal building is situated on the north side of the road. From the outside, this building has nothing in common with any preconceived, romantic images that you might associate with the term "trading post." Stop and go inside. Imagine that you are living in this part of New Mexico. You don't want to drive to Gallup or Grants. What do you need for your daily life? Chances are what you want is here at the Lewis Trading Post.

Past the trading post you will see signs directing you to such diverse places as Sunset Village, the Navaho Housing Authority, Navaho Estates, and Timber Lake. Take any of these roads and go for a wanderer's side trip. The main road will be waiting for you when you return.

Be sure to notice the corrals at the turnoff to Timber Lake. These corrals are a statement of human ingenuity and opportunism. Whoever built the corrals used the natural pockets in the up-thrust rock ridge as shelter for the animals. It is a simple yet ingenious way of providing shelter without buliding any. The ridge also provides a natural wall for the corrals. It seems an obvious thing to do yet I wonder if I would have thought of it, if I had not seen this one?

Continue down New Mexico 53 until you reach Ramah, New Mexico. This little town appears to be a prosperous farming community and it is. There are groves of narrow-leafed cottonwood trees and wide, shady streets. The houses are tidy and the lawns all seem to have been recently mowed. The town has an exacting neatness that is sometimes lacking in small towns.

Ramah was founded in 1874 by a group of Mormon settlers who named their town after a character in the Book of Mormon. The post office was established in 1884 and Ramah has been flourishing ever since. Close to the Ramah Trading Post in the center of town, you can see the old Masters Brothers Trading Post. This trading post is closed now but it does coincide with a more romantic idea of what a trading post should look like. This trading post, built of light-colored, quarried stone with a solid, lasting look to it, has two impressive stone towers on either side of the front door. It is easy to imagine a big freight wagon loaded with goods pulled up to the outside or a team hitched to the rail in front.

If you can't imagine this scene, you might want to visit Sheryl and Keith Clawson of Ramah. Between 1902 and 1916, Keith's grandfather, Fred Lewis, photographed the people, places, and events in this part of New Mexico, including photographs of the old Masters Brothers Trading Post in its heyday. Fred Lewis also took pictures of the community life of Ramah, and recorded the logging camps and timber industry in the Zuni Mountains. His photographs show tools, clothes, and methods of work that are gone or obsolete. Whether Fred Lewis was an artist taking images from the world around him, a historian preserving a certain time and life in New Mexico, or an avid amateur dabbling in the latest technology of his time, is not known. What he left behind was a small, open window. Looking through that photographic window, you can see the past.

When Sheryl and Keith Clawson found Fred Lewis's collection of glass negatives, they set out to learn whatever they could about that type of photographic process. Eventually they were able to start printing photographs from the old glass plates. The Clawsons are interested in sharing Fred Lewis's photographic art. They make and sell prints from the old negatives for whoever is interested. Some of the Clawsons' prints are hanging in the Grants District Ranger Station, some in a restaurant in Grants, and some are reproduced in this book. If you are interested in Fred Lewis's photographs and would like a memento from the past, contact Keith Clawson, P.O. Box 163, Ramah, New Mexico, 87321. This is a hobby with the Clawsons and they work on it when they have time, so don't expect immediate service from these people.

Leave Ramah on New Mexico 53 and head west to Zuni Pueblo, a short trip of less than twenty miles. This section of New Mexico 53 was once an army supply route between Fort Union in north-central New Mexico and Fort Defiance on the eastern Arizona border. During the 1850s it took an army pack train about two weeks to travel between the two forts. As a regular army supply route, this section of road was the scene of one of the oddest events in the history of the West.

During the mid-1850s, the top officials in the United States Army decided that the hot western deserts were exacting too great a toll on the horses, mules, and oxen used there. The U.S. Army decided to experiment with other modes of transportation. The upshot of this top-flight military thinking was the Great U.S. Army Camel Experiment. Reasoning that a desert was a desert, the U.S. Army imported a herd of Bactrian camels (the two-hump variety) to be used as pack animals in the western desert forts. Accompanying the camels was a camel driver from Syria. Although the camels were intended for work in the Arizona desert, they also traveled on the army trail that today is New Mexico 53.

The army's camel experiment was a success. The camels could and did out-perform oxen, horses, and mules. Nonetheless, the army abandoned the camel project with the beginning of the Civil War, and orders were given to have all of the camels liberated in the Arizona desert. Left to their own resources, the camels did not thrive. Essentially domesticated beasts that could not fend for themselves very well, they fell prey to the curious, the hunters, and the hungry. They terrified the desert wanderers who came upon them, ignorant of their history.

Eventually all of camels vanished from the desert. The camel driver, who had been abandoned along with the Great Camel Experiment, did not. This man, known as Hadji Ali, did well in the American West. Hadji Ali is said to have been a tall and handsome man with an irresistible flair. The English-speaking residents of the Arizona Territory corrupted his name to Hi-Jolly and welcomed him. He was known to be a good man with livestock and a hard-working individual. Some of the residents of the hospitable West took him to their hearts and today Hi Jolly's many descendents are living in Arizona. The last camel

Zuni Pueblo, 1910. In the past, Zuni did not have the structural outlines of a traditional pueblo. (Photo © Sheryl and Keith Clawson. Used by permission).

was seen in 1910, but Arizona cowboys are still singing old songs about the wrangler from the Far East.

ZUNI PUEBLO AND BLACK ROCK

As you enter the Zuni Indian land, you might prepare yourself for a few surprises. The Zunis are a unique group of Indians. Although they have lived in a town or pueblo for hundreds of years, they are not related to the pueblo-dwelling Indians along the Rio Grande Valley. They have a unique language and a unique culture. Furthermore, their town today looks nothing like the Pueblo towns of Taos, Acoma, or Santo Domingo. Zuni and its accompanying suburb of Black Rock are different.

Just as you pass the turnoff to New Mexico 602, pull off the road at the rest area and look at the country. The Rio Pescado will be running past you on the north. Cottonwoods growing along the Rio will be waving their graceful limbs. The amaranth will be standing

Zuni, 1988. The outlines of the pueblo have been altered by time and technology.

tall by the roadside and there will be red cliffs in the background. Whether you are there in the spring or the fall, the colors and forms you can see from this quiet roadside stop are artistic and striking.

Back on New Mexico 53, drive on toward Black Rock. This community looks very much like every housing development in America. You will be able to see paved bike paths and a jogging trail. There are sidewalks, volleyball courts, and gardens. Houses with satellite dishes edge the carefully laid out streets. This may not fit the cliché "Indian Village" but it is definitely the image of American working people of the twentieth century.

Past Black Rock, the wide street will take the traveler on to Zuni. It will also take the traveler past video rental stores, chile parlors, hamburger stands, curio and gift shops, broasted chicken stands, and a football field. Welcome to Zuni Pueblo.

Zuni is not an adobe pueblo. In the past it did have the structural outlines of a traditional pueblo but these have been softened by time and technology. The traveler gets the idea that many of the buildings in Zuñi are made of stone, not adobe bricks. There are few of the maintenance-hungry, flat roofs. In their place are pitched roofs of galvanized metal or shingles. The old-fashioned homes stand side-by-side with the more recent ones, and modern architecture competes with traditional. You get the idea that there is room for change and growth in Zuni Pueblo, and that the past has not been thrown away.

Because of their location on the Rio Pescado (Spanish for "river with many fish") and their proximity to Mexico, the Zunis were visited by almost all of the famous and infamous conquistadores and explorers. When the Spanish heard tales of the rich town located on the banks of *el rio pescado*, they immediately thought of gold. It might not have occurred to them that "rich" meant a town with plenty of water in the river, plenty of game in the nearby mountains and plenty of crops growing in the irrigated fields. On hearing that Zuni was a rich town, the Spaniards assumed it was one of the fabled Seven Cities of Gold, one of the Seven Cities of Cibola. Their location made the Zuni villages among the first Native American settlements the Spanish came to when traveling north out of Mexico. When the conquistadores found no gold or treasure at Zuni, they pressed on, optimistically figuring that the gold and riches must be in the *next* town, farther north.

In 1581, one of the Spanish missionaries gave the Zunis a flock of sheep that was later stolen by the Navahos, who, after many wild and tragic adventures with the United States government, eventually became shepherds and weavers. As time went by, the Navahos became known as the most talented and artistic weavers among the Native Americans of the Southwest.

The Zunis, meanwhile, did not become known for their sheep-raising prowess. They learned the art of silversmithing, as did many of the Native Americans in the region. For the most part, the early Zuni smiths made jewelry for themselves and their families. Only occasionally did they trade it for something else.

In the late 1920s, the railroad and mining boom came to this part of New Mexico. The Anglos wanted Indian jewelry and the Zunis began to expand their trade circles. They were at a disadvantage, however. They lived close to Gallup and many of the other Native American bands were also trading their silver and turquoise jewelry there. At this time, there was not a great diversity in style among the Native American silversmiths. Much of the jewelry was similar because all of the silversmiths had the same tools, the same materials, and the same teachers.

The Zunis needed an advantage, and under the guidance of an Anglo trader named G. C. Wallace and another Gallup trader named Katy Noe, they began to develop a style of silver jewelry that was to become uniquely theirs. This evolving style consisted of jewelry set with many tiny, tiny turquoise stones, often no larger than an eighth of an inch long. Each stone was individually carved to shape and set into tiny silver frames, or bezels, arranged in graceful geometric patterns. The designs of the minute stones were so delicate and fine that they reminded many people of the tiny stitches in needlepoint tapestries. Thus, this style of jewelry came to be known as Zuni needlepoint. The Zunis are still making this distinctive style of jewelry today.

The Zunis are also famous for their ability to carve fetishes. Most of the Zuni fetishes are animals and birds. According to legend, at one time the world was not dominated by mankind but instead belonged to the animals, who were more powerful than they are today. A disaster overtook this world and all of the animals were changed to stone. In later times, when mankind was introduced into the world, times were hard. Humans were weak and needed help. Occasionally, a sharp-eyed person would discover one of the old stone animals. The stone animal would be carefully carried to a home, ritually cared for, offered food, and asked for help. Even in its altered state, one of these old, powerful animals could help the people.

The Zunis became skilled in removing the stone surrounding the old animals and bringing out their animal shape. They became stone carvers. Today the Zunis produce very fine sculpture done on a delicate scale. Much of it is commercial and is sold as such, but tradition persists. Some Zunis still find the powerful old animals in the stones. These animals are respected and cared for, fed and offered tobacco to smoke. People are still weak and need help, and good help is very hard to find these days.

Much of the information about Zuni traditions and the Zuni past was gathered and recorded by Frank Hamilton Cushing. In 1879, Cushing was sent by the Smithsonian Institute to Zuni Pueblo. He accompanied the Stevenson collecting party as the ethnologist. After riding by mule from Las Vegas, New Mexico, he reached Zuni Pueblo and his adventures began.

Little by little his patience and sensitivity earned him the friendship and trust of the Zunis. Little by little, the Zunis worked at turning him into one of their own. Eventually he was living in their pueblo, wearing only Zuni attire, and eating Zuni food. Cushing learned the language of the pueblo and became not just an accepted member of the community, but a citizen, a Zuni.

Much of what Cushing wished to sketch and write down was considered secret and sacred by the Zunis. He gained permission to accomplish his research by explaining that the white man felt the Zunis and other Southwestern Indians had *no* religion and it would be worthwhile to inform them and cure their ignorance. Cushing spent the rest of his career in the Southwest on this task. It is possible that much of Zuni tradition and history would have been lost to the passage of time if Cushing had not been around to collect and write about it.

Tradition persists at Zuni Pueblo. I went there once as a casual tourist and was turned away. The people were practicing their old religion. They did not want sightseers and tourists around. I was told politely and firmly to return on another day.

Another day did come. I went to Zuni for a feast day. There was a parade and a dance, a fun run, and the Zunis were all out and about, dressed in their fine traditional clothing and swathed in their best jewelry. Their neighbors from Gallup and the pueblos in the north were there, too, as well as tourists and anthropologists from all over. It was a boisterous, happy crowd and there was a good feeling in the air. You could buy cotton candy and fresh tamales. The Zuni ladies had set up their tables and were offering the visitors handcrafts of every kind—pottery, needlepoint silver jewelry, beadwork, fetishes. You could also buy fresh corn, melons, chile, and squash. You could hear drums in the distance and rock-and-roll on the boom boxes carried by the teenagers. People threaded their way through the crowds on horseback and rolled by in campers. It was a true holiday, a real feast day.

I stopped at a table to look at some of the pottery and found a storyteller figure. A storyteller is a grandmother or grandfather figure sitting down with legs stretched out in front, mouth open, in the act of telling a story. Perched on its knees, arms, and legs, clinging to its back, sides, and chest are many, many tiny figures representing all of the children who have heard the stories. I bought the story teller and the Zuni grandmother who took my money and wrapped it in newspapers cautioned me to be careful and not to break the "babies." I carried it gently.

I stopped at the glossy arts-and-crafts gallery and looked at the items there. The carpeting was deep and the glass display cases were artfully lighted. Well-dressed, articulate salespeople stood behind each case. I admired the frog fetishes. The salesman told me that frogs were connected to Zuni religion and were part of the old superstitions. Frogs were supposed to be instrumental in bringing rain. I purchased a small black frog to remind me of my day at Zuni Pueblo. It was a feast day about rain, anyway.

At my home, the frog went to live on a shelf. He looked rather out of place there so I gave him a piece of turquoise for company. I wondered if he was a true stone frog, a frog from the other time, when animals were more powerful. How was one to know? If he was a true stone frog, he must be very uncomfortable living on a city shelf. I gave him a pinch of cornmeal in apology and stroked his smooth black head. It rained. I wondered.

THE ROAD TO GALLUP

Leave Zuni Pueblo and drive out New Mexico 53 heading east. When you reach New Mexico 602, turn left onto this road and drive north to Gallup. This is another perfect road for the motorcycle enthusiast. It is smooth, wide, and flat. Usually it is free of traffic. The air is clean of city pollutants. The scenery is inviting. Gallup is about 22 miles away.

Cedar and piñon flourish here. It is rugged land with great buttes of rock swinging arms down toward the road. Among the rock arms are small stands of ponderosa pine. Grindelia, or gumweed, blooms golden on the roadside. Grey-green bushes of Mormon tea extend spiky branches to the sky. As you drive along this road, you will not see cattle in fields or old abandoned cars pushed into arroyos. You will see the same vignette repeated over and over. You will see the homes of prosperous Navahos. Many of these people have moved from their original homes on the big reservation to this area, in order to be close to their jobs in Gallup. They have not moved into the town. They have relocated to this section of the reservation that is like a suburb of Gallup.

At each of these home places you will see groups of buildings: rectangular houses, barns, and outbuildings. Somewhere among all of the angular boxes will be a round or hexagonal hogan with a curving roof. These homes are large enough for an extended family; there is always room enough for an old aunt, a nephew, and a sister. The livestock here is usually horses, dogs, and chickens. The traditional herd of sheep is not in sight. In order to keep sheep, there must be a shepherd and the traditional shepherds are all in school at Gallup.

At each home place there is a blend of the modern with the old-fashioned, the archaic. Every home has a television antenna on the roof and many have a satellite dish in the yard. You can see basketball hoops and nets nailed up on posts and barns. Sometimes they share the post with an electric security light. Along with every satellite dish and basketball hoop, there will be stacks of wood for stoves and fireplaces. Some of the wood will be chopped into stove lengths but most of it will be arranged in huge, conical woodpiles that may be unusual to the person raised in other regions. In a vertical woodpile, the logs are placed on end and leaned against each other, making a conical, tee-pee shape. This is a very practical arrangement. In the spring and summer, this kind of woodpile eliminates the convenient hidey-holes for snakes and rodents that are characteristic of horizontal wood stacks. In the fall and winter, this type of wood stack is rarely buried by snow. It is easy to wiggle out a single log, let it drop to the ground and chop it up. This is a woodstack that one person can manage. It takes up less space than conventional woodpiles of chopped and neatly stacked logs. And it's traditional; what more could one ask except for the sight of a plume of grey smoke coming out of a stovepipe and the scent of burning piñon in the cold air?

This collection of buildings, satellite dishes, woodpiles, and animals will be repeated in every little canyon and draw you drive past. You will also see numerous missions, mission schools, and aluminum-can hunters. Some aspects of civilization will always be with us.

The other inevitable aspect of life in this part of the world is mud. There is no paving once you leave the highway, no sidewalks connecting the main houses with the barns, horse corrals, or traditional log hogans. There is a tremendous amount of cliche clay, red dirt, adobe soil waiting for enough water to turn into sticky, gooey, oozy, clinging mud. The greatest contradiction in the Southwest is that a land that is so starved for water should be so troubled by mud. When you see a powerful pickup truck mired in the mud, you are not just seeing a stuck truck. You are seeing total frustration. When you see a graceful woman wearing pretty, fashionable clothes but strong, sensible shoes, you are not seeing a woman without an eye for tasteful accessories; you are seeing a way of life. Life with mud.

Drive on to Gallup, New Mexico. A different view of life awaits the wanderer there.

GRANTS TO GALLUP

ON OLD ROUTE 66

REMEMBERING FRANK ARNOLD

As you leave Grants and drive west to Gallup, it is fitting that you remember Frank Arnold. You are following in his tracks. Frank Arnold, according to his daughter, who lives in Ramah, New Mexico, was the first person to drive onto Route 66 on the day that highway was officially opened in New Mexico. Frank Arnold, wanderers in New Mexico salute you! Thanks for showing us the way!

Two miles outside of Grants you will come to Milan, New Mexico. This small town was not named for the city in Italy. It was named for Salvador Milan, founder of the village and longtime mayor. Salvador Milan was also the brother of Mrs. Gunn, of cafe fame in Cubero.

THE CARROT FIELDS

Leaving Milan, you will begin to notice that the land is extraordinarily flat. It is unnaturally level. It is very dry. What meets your eyes today makes it very difficult to believe that in the late thirties and forties, all of this land was green with truck farming. You are driving through the old carrot fields of New Mexico.

These carrot fields once extended for approximately twelve miles west of Grants. Carrrot farming was a very big, very prosperous business until the beginning of the 1950s. Although the story is inaccurate, the wanderer will often hear that the carrot empire folded because the uranium companies bought the water rights from the carrot growers. Without the water, the desert quit blooming with carrots and went back to being a desert again. In actuality, the uranium boom did not start up in the Grants-Milan area until the late part of the fifties, and the carrots had been gone for more than ten years by then.

"I'll never forget the first time I saw the carrot fields of Grants. It was in 1945. They tell me that some sights can change your life, or at least your point of view. I think the carrot fields did that. They filled me with awe. They made me realize what water can do. They made me think of New Mexico as a sleeping field, just waiting for enough water to wake it up and turn it into a great green empire. Of course, that might never happen. There probably isn't enough water to do that for all the desert land, but there was enough for those carrot fields. Those fields were so green. They looked so soft and alive compared to the desert surrounding them, compared to the desert I had just driven through. Dotted among all of the greenery were little bright specks of color: orange, red, and purple. Colors that shone in the sun were moving around in the fields: yellow, black and pink. Even the grey specks were sort of luminescent. All of those colors were the velvet shirts of the Navahos, who were picking those carrots by hand.

Those carrot fields covered thousands of acres between Grants and Bluewater. Those carrots were the base of a financial empire and most of the work was done by hand and done by the Navaho. Those carrots were planted, cultivated and pulled, mostly by manual labor.

Those carrrots were shipped out by railroad. There weren't any refrigerated cars then; everything perishable had to be packed in ice. Eventually, the carrot business got so big that a modern ice plant was built in Grants, near the railroad tracks, right by the old roundhouse, right where the Diamond G Home Center is now. It was a big facility that could make ice, chip ice, and then blow it into the railroad cars filled with carrots. Those cars, everyone called 'em reefers, would speed along the tracks to St. Louis and chicago and you could see the water dripping out of them as that ice melted.

Then they built a big box factory next to the ice plant. Everyone had jobs there. The Indians would pull the carrots and load them onto a horse-drawn wagon and take them to the washing sheds near the fields. Then the clean carrots would be taken over to the railroad siding and packed into boxes or packed into the reefers. They'd blow in the chipped ice and then all of the carrots would be gone, east and west. You know, it takes two years to grow a carrot. The whole enterprise was a wonderful success story, a remarkable business and it lasted many years.

In the late forties those little plastic bags appeared. You could put carrots in them and they would stay fresh without ice. It was just like now. You didn't need to pack carrots into special boxes from the box factory. You didn't need to cover them with chipped ice from the ice plant. Just load them up on a wagon in the field and take them to the washing shed. Wash them, bag them, and there you were. No boxes, no ice.

I regretted the end of the carrot fields. I used to look forward to driving through Grants at dusk. There was a collection of small hogans for the workers that you could see from route 66. It was a sort of company town, I guess. I imagine that the living conditions might not have been the best. But it was so peaceful to look away from the highway to that scattering of little round houses. Each one had a small piñon fire in front and you could see the Indian ladies in their long graceful skirts, cooking dinner over their bright little fires. Those people had work and food and shelter. Their little piñon fires shone so brightly in the dim light. It couldn't have been all bad."

The Peddler wasn't the only one who liked the carrot fields in Grants. My grandmother loved the carrots. She used to love to see the trucks come into Albuquerque from Grants. Those trucks would be loaded with carrots, with hundreds of feathery carrot tops drooping from the back of the truck.

"Pull in behind that one, Alan!" she would encourage my grandfather if they spotted a Grants produce truck on the Albuquerque streets. "I want to look at those carrots!" she would declare firmly. My grandfather would obligingly maneuver the old family sedan behind the carrot truck. My grandmother, an avid gardener whose thumbs were green all the way to her elbows, would inspect the Grants carrots with a keen and critical eye. "I'm going to grow some like that, this year," she would announce. Though she tried many varieties, she was never satisfied that she was growing the same high quality carrots as those that came to Albuquerque from the Grants carrot fields.

Ten miles out of Grants will find you are still driving through the former carrot fields.

When you begin to see stray buildings, homes, and businesses you will be approaching Bluewater Village. Start looking on the left side of the road for the old Bluewater Trading Post, a long building with big windows. In earlier times it was a major trading post and a classic example of a Route 66 tourist trap, but it's out of business now. The large murals that decorate the facade are beautiful specimens of the large-scale art that was once found on the outside walls of every trading post and tourist trap fronting Route 66. I don't know why these particular pictures look so fresh and bright, unless they have been recently painted. It don't know who painted them. If you are interested in art of the people, this is an art show you should not miss.

The Bluewater Trading Post seems to be in wrack and ruin. The last time I went there to see the murals it appeared that the building was being used for some type of Christian school or mission. The people in charge had posted a large ecumenical sign outside the front doors announcing, "We love everybody!" That type of announcement always gives a wanderer something to ponder.

"There were always a couple of trading posts operating in this area in the forties and fifties. I can remember the Bluewater Trading Post and Bowlin's particularly well. I used to call on them. You could visit those trading posts and sort of hang around and sooner or later someone would come in and start to talk about the cockfights. I guess cockfighting is illegal or maybe it is just illegal to bet on them but it was a big sport in this part of the world, at one time. Maybe it still is, I don't know. I saw the cockfights and I thought it was a real industry. Many men had invested thousands of dollars in those fighting roosters and some of them got a handsome return on their money. People would travel around, taking their best fighters to remote places where they had heard of a particularly fierce rooster. I guess it was bloody sometimes and the birds did get hurt, but if you grew up around chickens you knew that roosters were always going to fight other roosters, anyway. It didn't matter if people were watching or not. I'm not arguing either for or against the morality of rooster fighting here, but I want to explain that it didn't seem wrong or reprehensible, it was just something that some people did. Some people went to dances, others went to rooster fights. Pick your pleasure.

Cockfighting did bring out the ingenuity in people. It wasn't all blood, money, and violence. It encouraged some people to invent and create things that otherwise might never have come into being. It's always interesting to see a person use his mind. What do you do if you have a tremendous fighting cock who is all talent and ambition and has no spurs? How do you give artificial respiration to a rooster who has quit breathing? I saw those problems solved by some mighty creative trainers. I was impressed by the solutions.

Maybe there is something about this part of the land that encourages illicit activity. I don't know. I used to stop at a cafe around here, somewhere between Grants and this Bluewater area. I liked the food, even though the place had some terrible name like Mom's or Grandma's or something similar that should have warned you away. I remember it was late summer and the World Series was about to be played. The waitress in this place was a pretty woman and she was signing up all of the travelers for a pool on who would win the pennant. I've forgotten now who was playing, but I was a sport in those days and the waitress was pretty so I made my contribution and waited to see if I would win. I heard the final score when I was in Gallup and I had won. I traveled back towards Grants in a couple of days and I stopped in that cafe to pick up my winnings. Well, it was the oldest story in the book. The pretty waitress had already left the cafe with all of the money and hit the highway, traveling down Route 66. But the point of all this is that not too long after this scam, the cafe went out of business. Everyone who traveled down 66 told the story to everyone else. No one wanted to stop at that place anymore, even if the road went right by it, the food was good, and the waitress was gone. Route 66 wasn't just a road, it was a community."

PREWITT

By the time you have driven twelve miles outside of Grants, you will be leaving the carrot fields behind. The blinking lights and tall white towers of a generating plant are now the most dramatic man-made feature on the landscape. The next town up ahead will be Prewitt, New Mexico, founded by Robert Prewitt, trader. For many years and at least two generations, the Prewitt family had a trading post here. The Prewitts supplied the local ranchers and traded with the Navahos.

The most outstanding feature in Prewitt today may be the Rodeo Grounds, which you can easily spot from the highway. If you see any activity there, be sure to stop. A rodeo in one of these small New Mexican towns is often a showcase for amazing ability and talent. You can learn more about cowboy skills and rodeoing from one of these smaller rodeos than from one of the big productions in a city coliseum. Try to find a seat by some spectator who looks like a non-tourist and listen to the informed commentary. No one can appreciate a cowboy's performance as much as another person who has cowboyed, too.

BLUEWATER LAKE

Prewitt is also the turnoff to Bluewater Lake, which you reach by heading south out of Prewitt on New Mexico State Road 412. Bluewater Lake is not a natural lake. A man-made reservoir created by damming the waters of Triangle Bar Spring and Azul Creek, it is said to be one of the best fishing spots in New Mexico. If you like fat lake trout, try your luck here.

Bluewater Lake was the dream of many men, yet many years passed before it became a reality. People first came to settle in the Bluewater Valley as early as 1850. It was plain to those first homesteaders that the main requirement for their success would be a steady, reliable source of water. A reservoir that would hold the water of the creeks and nearby springs seemed to be the answer, and in 1885, a dam was built. It was a dirt-fill dam and it washed away in 1886. After the failure of the dirt dam, the homesteaders made other attempts to create an irrigation system for the Bluewater Valley, but nothing was successful, and the drought of 1891 finished off all attempts at homesteading in the valley. No one could farm the semi-arid land without a reliable source of water.

In 1894, a new group of settlers decided to try farming the area. A new dam was built across the Bluewater Valley and the settlement there acquired an air of permanence, even though the possibility of the dam breaking remained a constant threat to the community. Eventually, the Atchison, Topeka and Santa Fe Railroad became interested in the community and the project to construct a safe dam. The company built a concrete dam in the Bluewater Valley and that one lasted until 1904, when it went the way of the previous dams and washed out. By this time, however, many people were living in the Bluewater Valley and a dam was a necessity for their livelihood. So the present dam was built. The reservoir grew to 20 square miles and the area surrounding it became a recreational site and then a state park.

The journey to Bluewater Lake is a very pleasant side trip, especially if you have a need to gaze at acres and acres of water. There are campsites and picnic facilities at the lake.

Back on Route 66/Interstate 40, you have a long, straight drive to the next town. Although the highway here is divided into four lanes with a generous median strip, the sights along the roadside have not changed very much since this part of the road was known as "66 to Gallup." Red mesas still edge the horizon, and herds of sheep and goats still wander picturesquely across the countryside. You can still see the traditional Navaho hogans in the distance, still round or six-sided with domed roofs, still built with their doors facing east.

Whizzing down the blacktop, you can still see billboards advertising a tourist trap up ahead that features "Real Indian Weavers!" or "Live Rattlesnakes!" Every so often a sign will pop up warning or cajoling wanderers about the state of their souls. These signs are invariably near a Christian mission or boarding school. The sheep, the hogans, the billboards, and the mission signs are much as they were in the halcyon days of Route 66. Some things don't change, or at least they change very slowly.

THOREAU

Thoreau is the next town on Route 66. This spot, started as a railroad station in the early days of the Atchison, Topeka and Santa Fe Railroad, was named for Henry David Thoreau, the American author and philosopher who was much acclaimed in the 1880s.

Although it was named for Henry David Thoreau, New Mexicans in the know never say "Thoreau." They say "Threw" or "Through." Sometimes New Mexicans even argue about the correct pronunciation of this small town's name. Those people who favor the "Threw" pronunciation know their grammar: Threw is the past tense of throw. Those who argue for the "Through" pronunciation are thinking practically: that's what most people do, when they get to Thoreau, they simply pass through the place. Although all of this may seem like a joke to some or a great deal of unncessary quibbling about a name, it is all deadly serious.

If you should ever meet anyone who claimed he or she was from New Mexico, but you had some doubts about it, you can use Thoreau as a quick test. Cleverly inquire if the stranger has ever stopped in the small town between Prewitt and the Continental Divide. If the stranger begins to talk about "Threw" or "Through," you can safely bet you have met a native New Mexican. It is interesting to note that none of this has anything to do with Henry David.

Thoreau is the home of the Frontier Trophy Buckle company. Frontier Trophy Buckles is owned by Ralph Maynard and makes those much-coveted belt buckles that are the traditional prizes at rodeos.

Trophy buckles are big (some approaching the size of saucers), shiny (gold, silver, or nickel), and hard to earn. You can't walk into a store and simply buy one. You win your trophy buckle by staying on a bronc, wrestling a steer, roping a calf or goat, or tying some wild critter and doing it better and faster than anyone else.

Trophy buckles are the stuff of dreams and not just the dreams of kids. Adult competitors on the professional rodeo circuit dream of winning a trophy buckle just as fervently as any kid. They want that buckle because it proclaims they are the best in their field, they can rope, ride, or wrestle faster and better than anyone else.

You might meet a graying man at a country club, a grocery store, or a livestock auction and see a cherished trophy buckle on his belt. If you ask about it, he might say something like, "Yeah, I got that at the Rodeo de Santa Fe when I was just twenty and riding broncs. I just never found anything better for my belt." And he never will. That moment, when he won the buckle, was a high point in his life. Not all the begging from a favorite child or grandchild will part the man from his buckle. He's secretly hoping that his kids or grandkids will go and win their own buckles, just like he did.

I've seen only one trophy buckle without an owner. I felt there must be some tragedy connected to it but I never found out the story. On a very bitter, very cold Sunday morning, I found a trophy buckle for sale at the Albuquerque Flea Market. It was tossed down on a table among an odd and sorry pile of junk. It was a beauty, as big as a saucer, silver and heart-shaped. It had tiny, four-petaled flowers along the edge and each little flower had a shiny red ruby or garnet in its center. It was engraved with scrolls and fancy flourishes and the lettering across it read "Sweetheart of the Rodeo." It was decorated with a running horse and coils of rope and a name engraved on it; the winner of this grand trophy was Starla June.

Starla June, what happened to make you part with your buckle? Was being the champion barrel racer not enough? Was being Sweetheart of the Rodeo incompatible with your later life? Did you run out of money? Didn't your dreams come true, Starla June? Whenever I sit in the box seats at the State Fair and watch the rodeo contestants, whenever I lean up against the fence rails and watch the old-timers at the Magdalena Fourth of July Rodeo, whenever I see a girl on a horse practicing the barrels in a field in Albuquerque's South Valley, I wonder, what are you doing now, Starla June? What are you doing at this very moment?

Thoreau used to be a small spot on the railroad line. It had no video rental shops, no flea markets, no mobile homes, no beauty shops, no car washes, no bingo games, no pawn shops. It had one big trading post that sold groceries, hardware, and soft goods. The trading post accepted pawn from the customers. It bought wool. There was a mission church. Thoreau was home to some people. It was a very small place.

SIDE TRIP TO CROWNPOINT

Twenty miles north of Thoreau is the place known as Crownpoint. Visiting Crownpoint is a provocative experience. If you are of a reflective turn of mind, visiting Crownpoint will give you much to consider. If reflective thinking is not your idea of enjoyment, you might want to schedule your trip to Crownpoint on one of the Friday nights when they are having a rug auction. Crownpoint is famous for these rug auctions in which many fine examples of hand-woven Navaho rugs are auctioned off to the public. By skipping the middleman, these fine rugs are sold for reasonable (not cheap!) and fair prices, with the money going directly to the weavers.

Leave Thoreau and head out on New Mexico State Road 57. The next twenty miles will take you on a good paved road across some stark and barren country. This good paved road is treacherous when it is covered with snow. Be sure to check the weather conditions as well as the road conditions before you start.

The land you are driving across presents a great contrast to much of the land that Route 66 travels through. From Grants to Gallup, on either side of that old highway is a profusion of shrubs, small trees, and other desert plants. There is almost nothing like that along State Road 57. This land is almost bare. Only the most recent, the hardiest plants soften the landscape. This is not the sparse beauty of the desert; this is something painful and man-induced. There is almost no vegetation at all. Was it all grazed away by animals? Did it die? Whenever I travel to Crownpoint and see this land, I have the same thought: Something ought to be done about this land. The land needs help. But I do not know what to do, who owns the land, or even how it got like this. I do not know what to do or whom to speak with, so in my ignorance, I do nothing. The land does not seem to be recovering.

The wildness of the land asserts itself very quickly. You have only to drive eight or ten miles out of Thoreau and the influence of the highway and the high-tech power of the century seems to diminish a little bit. The cliffs on either side of the road are very red, and the dirt is not merely a rusty red but an actual red-red. In a metaphysical sense, the landscape itself seems to exude some force. It is very unusual country.

CROWNPOINT AND THE RUG AUCTIONS

Most of the economy of Crownpoint is centered around the Navaho Nation and most of the Crownpoint residents are, naturally, Navaho. Crownpoint is one of the Regional Headquarters of the Navaho Tribe, so many services provided for the tribal members are located here. There is a hospital, a modern vocational skills center, a junior and senior high and elementary school, as well as all of the accompanying bureaucracies needed to administer all of these services. There are also some Bureau of Indian Affairs offices here. The relationship between the tribe and the BIA is labyrinthine. In spite of its seemingly small size, a great many people live and work in Crownpoint.

Crownpoint also has its share of gas stations, convenience stores, fried chicken stands, hamburger places, and ice cream shops. Crownpoint also has churches, Boy Scout troops, athletic teams, joggers, rodeo participants, skate boarders, and bicyclists. In short, Crownpoint has everything that every other small town in America has.

What Crownpoint has that no other town has is the Crownpoint Rug Weavers Association and the association's regular rug auctions. There are several reasons why this is so unusual.

In the past, Navaho weavers produced blankets, saddle pads, and clothing for themselves and their families. The weavers were almost always women. Although a few men knew about weaving, they were the exception and usually weavers only through special circumstances. The most notable of these men was Hosteen Klah, a *haa'taali* or medicine man, who began to weave as a way to preserve his knowledge of ceremonial sandpaintings.

At the beginning of the twentieth century, the Navaho weavers began to sell their rugs to traders who in turn sold them to tourists, gift shop owners, and art galleries. The traders are still the traditional outlet for the Navaho weavers. The small amount of money a weaver might receive depended on the trader and on the weaver's ability to drive a bargain, presuming the amount was a fair return for the product. The trader then sold the weavings at a higher price because he was in business and had expenses that the weaver did not. The gift shop owners and gallery operators who bought from the traders then raised the prices on the rugs and sold them again to their customers. The result of passing through so many hands was that, although Navaho rugs began to command very high prices, the weavers did not share in the prices their own textiles could command. (As a note of interest, many tourists and visitors to the Southwest who purchased rugs and take them home, often decide that the rugs are too barbaric or too strong to mix with their home decor. The weavings are then put away in mothballs, and forgotten. When the original purchaser dies, the weavings are discovered, often in museum quality condition and are appraised and sold at the extremely high market value. By this time, the original weaver of the rug has been forgotten and so she still does not benefit from the high prices that her reputation might now command.)

All of this is extremely elementary economics. The Crownpoint rug weavers came up with an equally elementary solution to the problem of other people benefitting more from their work than they were. Their solution, however simple, represented a radical departure from tradition.

The rug weavers, under extraordinary leadership, formed an association. This was a radical departure because the rug weavers had always operated as independent businesswomen, each one dealing with the traders to the best of her ability. Naturally, some weavers were not as good at this as their sisters and so received even lower prices for their equally fine craftswomanship. As a collective, the rug weavers had more control over their products. They opted to skip the traders and sell their rugs directly to buyers at auction. This way, they could benefit directly from the current high market price for Native American art. They could also retain their status as independent businesspeople.

The Crownpoint Rug Weavers Association now sponsors almost monthly rug auctions in Crownpoint. Each weaver may submit rugs to be auctioned and each weaver determines the reserve or minimum price that she will accept for her work. Under this system, the weavers decide their own destiny. They are not put in a position to be taken advantage of if they are not good at wrangling with prospective buyers. The wrangling is left to an auctioneer hired by the association, whose professional responsibility it is to get the best price he can for his clients. If the crowd of buyers will not meet the reserve, nobody loses and the rug still belongs to the weaver.

Besides the equity of the rug auction system, the Crownpoint Rug Auctions are fun and fascinating to attend. They are held in one of the school gyms and they are always on a Friday evening. If you want to witness the entire system at work, however, the action usually starts about three in the afternoon when the weavers begin to show up with their rugs. Each rug is checked in, tagged with a number and the weaver's name and put on display on large tables set up in the gym. At this time, the weaver will declare her reserve. This amount is not put on the identifying tag but is recorded for the auctioneer.

Once the rug is checked in and put on display, the spectators can examine it, compare it to other rugs, measure it, judge its quality and in general, just go shopping. Browsing through the piles of rugs is one of the most fascinating and frustrating experiences that a textile buff can have. There are always so many to see that you give up hope of seeing them all. Every rug that you examine has a beauty of its own. Even if you have no intention of buying a rug, you become absorbed in the process of comparing, judging and choosing. You find yourself writing down the numbers of your favorite rugs, just in case the bidding happens to fall in your price range.

When your mind is reeling with designs and colors, it is time to stop looking at the rugs and turn your attention to your fellow spectators and rug shoppers. Some of them are methodical rug examiners. They record rug numbers in notebooks instead of on matchbook covers. They are often dressed in western clothes, Stetsons, and much silver jewelry. These people may be professional buyers who can and will spend thousands of dollars at the evening auction and return to Albuquerque, Phoenix, or Tucson with a load of rugs for a shop or a gallery. You can also see tourists, citizens of Crownpoint, and visitors from other countries of the world. You may see a flamboyant interior decorator, fulfilling every stereotype you ever cherished about that profession. You may spot an anthropologist taking field notes or a photographer taking pictures.

Perhaps the most interesting rug browsers of all are the rug weavers themselves. These ladies stand quietly in line, waiting to register their rugs. They bring their works rolled up in flour sacks, paper bags, or sheets of plastic. After they have passed through the registration line, they go to the big tables themselves to see what their sister craftswomen have produced. These ladies are dignified. They converse with a friend or a daughter in quiet voices. They pass strong hands gently over the woolen rugs, touching a design, hefting the weight. Their attitude seems to be one of curious, professional interest. You rarely see frowns or big grins, but they seem to be pleased to examine and compare the rugs, the wealth of effort spread out on the big tables.

All of this is quiet, low-key drama. Loud voices are the exception until the children begin to show up. School is out for the day and boisterous youngsters begin joining their mothers and looking for grandmothers who have driven in from a remote homesite for the Friday evening event. Kipling may have written about the cultural clash between East and West, but he never attended a Crownpoint rug auction. He never saw a small Navaho boy with a crewcut share a snack of Colonel Sanders' fried chicken with an elderly Navaho lady in a full, traditional, ankle-length skirt. He never saw that same small boy get up from the meal, pick up his skateboard and start playing on the sidewalk, circling the American flag in front of the school while uttering karate cries and tugging on the bottom of his Coca-Cola t-shirt. Kipling didn't see this boy's grandmother smile at him with love and approval while he did tricks for her on his skateboard. Kipling didn't see this same lady standing in front of a glass display case in the hallway of the school, looking at the same small boy's prize-winning essay. Sometimes cultures do not clash. Sometimes, in lucky times, the old and the new blend.

Outside the school in the parking lot, pickup trucks are filling up the parking spaces. Old friends and neighbors are standing in bunches, or sitting in the beds of the trucks exchanging news and visiting. On the tailgates of some trucks are big kettles and coolers. Out of these come tamales, cupcakes, or *bah doolklizi*, a flat round cake made from blue cornmeal, water, and juniper ashes. All of these are for sale and a wanderer can make a good meal from the offerings of the pickup trucks.

If you desire a more formal meal, the school cafeteria usually sells a hot Navaho taco dinner about five o'clock. A Navaho taco is a round piece of puffy, deep-fat fried dough that covers your dinner plate. Heaped on top are lettuce, tomatoes, cheese, and pinto beans. Sometimes the beans are hot and spicy in a meat and chile broth and sometimes they are plain beans. The contents of the Navaho taco depend a great deal on the cook. Navaho tacos are always good. Navaho tacos are always hot, salty, crispy, and filling. Navaho tacos are a cross between three cooking traditions. Navaho tacos are real food.

Around five o'clock, the action begins to pick up. People are finished with work for the week and they begin to gather. In the hallways of the school, people are setting up card tables. Cub Scout mothers, PTA mothers, and mother mothers are getting ready for the crowd. Soon you can buy hot dogs, egg rolls, brownies, cupcakes, cookies, and pie from the different groups raising money. Someone starts popping corn and that carnival smell fills the air. Other people are carefully arranging pottery, beadwork, and silver jewelry on tabletops covered with bright Pendleton blankets. Children giggle and play up and down the halls. Parents chase them outdoors. Men in Stetsons lean up against the walls and talk. Teenagers eye each other and go through familiar teenage rituals.

People begin to drift into the gym. The big tables of rugs are gone and in their place are rows of folding chairs. Up in front, the auctioneer's stage is set up and the microphone is tested. Bookkeepers and assistants in western shirts and cowboy hats arrange themselves on either side of the stage.

Finally the auction begins. Each rug is held up for the audience by two of the auctioneer's assistants. The weaver's name and home area are announced. The rug number is read out and the bidding begins. Some rugs are greeted with applause for an excellent design or unusual size. Some are not. The auctioneer adds comments and tells the crowd if the weaver is exceptionally young and a beginner or perhaps is an older lady with still-skillful hands.

The pace is steady. Buyers go up to the tables on either side of the auction block to pay for their rugs as soon as the bidding is finished. Hours slip by. The clock is saying ten and everyone breaks for coffee and baked goods from the tables in the hall.

The bidding resumes. The auction will not stop until every rug has been shown. Children fall asleep on blankets and shawls that have been spread on the floor. The noise level falls, too. The crowd is a little thinner. Out in the hall you can hear the old rumor about how the stingy are waiting for a late hour in order to get a cheaper price. I've heard this at every rug auction I've been to but I could never see that it was true. Even at one in the morning, the steady singsong of the auctioneer is commanding your attention and working for the rug weavers.

The last rug is shown, bid on, and sold. Thanks are offered all around. Announcements about the next auctions are repeated and everyone gets ready to go home. Trucks are packed, sleepy children are carrried out, and glimmering headlights shine over dark roads. The people are driving home to Mariano Lake and Pine Dale, White Horse, and Hospah, Mexican Springs, and Naikibito.

You get into your car and cradle your rug in your arms. You bought the best one. The wool is stiff but not hard if you rub your cheek against it. Navaho rugs do not drape. You think you can see the colors in the pattern when the stars and moon shine through the windshield. You hold a piece of time and knowledge in your hands. The rug weaver has her own satisfaction, too. You wonder if she has plans for another rug, maybe a bigger one, maybe with different colors. Did she see you pay for her rug? Will she ever know how you treasure her efforts? What plans does she have for the money that went from your hands to hers? Will it go for more yarn? A truck payment? Food for her family? A skateboard for a little boy?

It's a long drive home. Nighttime thoughts fill every truck and car. The rug weaver and the rug buyer travel the desert in different directions, moving farther and farther apart, under the wide sky.

CHACO CANYON SIDE TRIP

Crownpoint is the jumping off point if you want to visit Chaco Canyon National Monument, the site of one of the most extensive Anasazi towns in the Southwest. The Anasazi (Navaho for "the Old Ones") were thought to have lived in this area from about the fourth to the twelfth centuries A.D. Opinions differ as to whether the various scattered building complexes were continuously inhabited as towns or pueblos or were used as ceremonial sites and merely inhabited for short periods of time. Anthropologists believe that the Chaco Canyon site could have been populated with up to 5,000 residents at one time. Since the buildings are scattered up and down the canyon, there was not a single large settlement of 5,000 people but rather a cluster of small towns or pueblos of 500 or 600 inhabitants. Naturally these figures are not exact. The problem of population projection in Chaco Canyon is complicated by ecology. Was there enough water, firewood, and food in the area to support a population of thousands? This is a thorny question and one that is still under discussion.

Chaco Canyon is also the place where the sun dagger was discovered on Fajada Butte. The sun dagger is an extremely accurate solar calendar system. This indicator of solstices and equinoxes as well as lunar cycles shows that the people of Chaco Canyon had a sophisticated knowledge of astronomy. Many of these solar calendars can still be found in the Southwest. They are rare but not unique. Many are hidden in pictographs, waiting for the wanderer to discover their meaning and purpose.

At Chaco Canyon there are guided tours of the ruins and a Visitors Center with exhibits and explanations of what is known about the area and people who once lived there. It is open all year, and you will find simple amenities such as camping grounds, restrooms, and picnic areas. Chaco Canyon is a terrific example of tax payers' money well spent. Chaco Canyon is also smack in the middle of a desert so if you go be sure and take a hat.

To go to Chaco Canyon, leave Crownpoint on Highway 57. The road is paved for the first fifteen miles, then turns to gravel and leads the wanderer across a stunning landscape of swooping buttes and red mesas. The landscape is vast and to a dweller of small spaces, it can be intimidating. Be brave; let yourself enjoy the openness.

Pay attention to the weather before you leave for Chaco Canyon. The last part of the trip on the gravel road can be hazardous if the road is wet with rain or snow. You will be in really remote country. Unless it is the peak tourist season in the summer, this is a lonely, untrafficked path.

From Chaco Canyon you may retrace your steps back to Crownpoint and return from there to Route 66. If you wish to explore the north, you can leave Chaco Canyon on a dirt road segment of New Mexico 57 and travel north to meet New Mexico 44. Once you are in this part of New Mexico, you have left the boundaries of this guidebook.

THE CONTINENTAL DIVIDE

Five miles west of Thoreau, you will arrive at the Continental Divide. When I was a child I was told with great seriousness that every river west of the Continental Divide flowed into the Pacific Ocean, that every drop of rain that fell west of the Continental Divide somehow found these streams and, joining them, made its way to the great ocean to the west. Likewise, all the rivers and moisture gathering east of the Divide eventually ended up in the Atlantic ocean. I thought about this for awhile and decided that the adults who told me this were either pulling my leg or repeating some well-worn myth in the same category as horsehair snakes. I come from a big family of tall-tale tellers and none of them are above deceiving a child with a wild story like the Continental Divide. They made me a wary cynic at an early age. This account of the Continental Divide seemed a little too pat for a natural phenomenon. Therefore it was to my utter chagrin when I found out in a geography class that something very like the account told to me as a child was actually happening on the North American continent.

The drive to the Continental Divide could wake up your cynicism. This stretch of highway is filled with many signboards advertising the delights of places to stop around the Continental Divide. Some of these signs are very old and are actually left over from the old days of Route 66. Some of them are newer. My favorite one advertises a trading post where everything is "50 percent off." It doesn't say off of what.

The Continental Divide is at an elevation of 7,275 feet. The town named for the backbone of the Rockies straggles along a half-mile strip and straddles the highway. Set against a breathtaking panorama of red cliffs, green piñons, blue skies, and white clouds, is a collection of bars, trading posts, tourist traps, and a dance hall. If you have time, you should stop at the Continental Divide and visit some of these places. One of the trading posts is still advertising an Indian weaver at work. Another has a great supply of horns from the Horn Man.

In the days when Route 66 was the major highway here, the biggest place to stop at the Continental Divide was a trading company called Top O' the World. In the forties, Top O' the World was a popular tourist stop since it combined a gas station with a trading post.

My mother was a young Old Maid Schoolteacher at this time and she often used to drive her old aunties from Phoenix to Albuquerque and back for their frequent family visits. Both coming and going, they always stopped at Top O' the World. There was always cold pop at the trading post and the trader there did a very big business with the local Indian weavers. He maintained a big rug room and my mother always liked to look through the rugs and see if she could come up with a bargain.

During one visit, my mother wandered into the rug room for a look around. She noticed a figure sitting on a pile of rugs in the back shadows but she didn't pay any attention to it. It was common for the trading post customers to lounge around the trading post while they waited for the trader or made up their minds about what they wanted.

My mother browsed from pile to pile of rugs and as she passed close to the figure, she saw that it was a wooden Indian, not a human being as she had originally thought. Intent on looking at the rugs, she paid no further attention to the carving and went on sorting through the weavings. As she glanced up while moving to another pile of rugs, she thought she saw the wooden Indian move. She looked at it intently but it was just a wooden Indian. It couldn't move. She turned back to the rugs and again she caught a flicker of movement from the figure. She whirled to catch it again but again there was only a wooden carving sitting on a pile of rugs. She glared at the life-size carving and the wooden Indian lifted its arm and waved at her. At the same time she heard a deep, masculine belly laugh. The trader emerged from behind a partition, convulsed with laughter and slapping his thighs in merriment. He pointed out the threads that ran from the wooden Indian's jointed arms to a spot behind the partition. "I've had more dern fun with this thing," he chortled, and my mother flounced out of Top O' the World, thoroughly miffed.

After World War II a radar site was built in the Continental Divide area, close to Top O' the World. This brought more money into the town and modernized things a bit. The soldiers stationed at the site would come to eat and drink at the bar and dance at the dance hall.

"Top O' the World used to be more than a trading post, you know. It used to be a nightclub or a honkytonk. They had pretty good food there, steaks and such, and some people would drive out from Gallup to eat there. It wasn't bad as places go, not a family place, but not too rough either. There was also a tourist court at Top O' the World and you probably could get any type of action there that you wanted.

Mostly I remember the music and the taxi dancers at Top O' the World. Those girls would work to charm you and get you to put nickels and dimes in the nickelodeon and dance with them. When you handed them the change so that they could choose a song, they would keep the money you gave them and drop their own silver in the slot, instead. Their money would be painted with fingernail polish and when the management emptied the machine, the painted money would be returned to the girls. The girls didn't live on the change they hustled for dancing. They also worked for the bar. After a dance, the girls would beg for a drink at the bar. The barman would serve the client a cocktail and the girl a coke and then charge you for two cocktails. Later on in the evening, the girl would get a split of that money, too. It always seemed like a tough way to make a living."

To some travelers of Route 66, Top O' the World was a sinister place. There was a dormitory there for the railroad workers and a boardinghouse, too. There wasn't much else besides those buildings, the bar, the dance hall, the trading post, and the tourist courts. It was fairly desolate country. Some people believed that the boardinghouse was a "sporting house" for the railroad workers and passing travelers but I have never been able to get the truth of that, one way or the other. Both the dormitory and the boardinghouse are gone today and the Continental Divide is a different place.

At this point, the original path of Route 66 merges with Interstate 40. As you continue to Gallup, you will see more signs advertising Christian mission schools and salvation. Suddenly, a monstrous Giant Travel Center will spring into view on the right-hand side of the road. If you have been wallowing in nostalgia, this sight will jar you back into the present. Unless you have some emergency and must stop here, pass it by. A visit to this ultra-modern, clean, interesting, well-supplied travel center will effectively banish all thoughts of Route 66 from your mind. On the other hand, if this is your kind of travel shop, put down this book, stop, and enjoy yourself.

Back on the road, you are approaching Gallup. At one time you would see Navahos walking along the road here, heading toward town. These people would not be hitchhiking; they would be simply traveling by foot. Today you rarely see that. Our world is dominated by cars.

FORT WINGATE

Up ahead is exit 33, which leads to Fort Wingate, a former U.S. Army post. Today an unmatched group of enterprises share the Fort Wingate address. The U.S. Army still maintains a post here called the Fort Wingate Military Reservation, which is primarily a large ordnance depot on 64,000 acres of land. Sharing this acreage is New Mexico's herd of American buffalo (*Bison bison*), part of a project to reestablish the species in North America. These animals are under the supervision of the New Mexico State Game and Fish Department. Close by is a different enterprise, a large boarding school and health facility for the Navaho Indians.

This is the third location for Fort Wingate. In 1850, this U.S. Army post was just north of Laguna, at Cebolleta, but in 1862 the post was moved to a location near Grants. In 1868, it moved to its present location just outside of Gallup. At that time an army post was already there, Fort Fauntleroy, named after its original commander, Col. Thomas T. Fauntleroy. With the advent of the Civil War, Fauntleroy left the U.S. Army to pursue his fortune with the Confederate forces. The army waited until 1866 and then renamed the facility Fort Lyon, which later merged with Fort Wingate, retaining the latter name. Benjamin Wingate was a captain in the Union Army who was killed in the 1862 Civil War battle at Valverde.

Today there are more changes ahead for Old Fort Wingate. At this writing, the military is making plans to close the post, and the State Game and Fish Department is making plans to reduce the buffalo herd that flourishes here. Buffalo will be sold to private breeding ranches and the herd will be thinned against the day that the army closes its reservation entirely.

Fort Wingate is interesting for another reason, one that you cannot see. In 1881, George Washington Matthews came here, one of the first, if not *the* first, anthropologists to study the people of the American Southwest. His curiosity about the Native Americans and their way of life was boundless. He wrote many papers for scholarly journals and popular magazines, detailing the food, shelter, clothing, and community customs of the indigenous people. While at Fort Wingate, Matthews persuaded a Navaho silversmith to "set up shop" and allow the anthropologist to watch and record the silversmithing process. Until this time, there had been no written account of this Navaho craft.

Silversmithing is not an ancient "Indian Art" in the Southwest. For a long time it was an art that belonged to the Mexican and Spanish inhabitants of the Rio Grande Valley. Since the Navahos spent a great deal of time and effort raiding, looting, and destroying the agricultural settlements of these people, there wasn't much opportunity for intercultural sharing of skills like silversmithing. In addition, the Navaho warriors did not possess the tools or the lifestyle that would lead them to develop and practice metalsmithing independently.

In 1853, a Navaho known as Herrero (Spanish for "the iron worker") or Atsìdì Sanì (Navaho for "the Old Smith") did learn the craft from some Mexican *plateros* (silversmiths). His career was short-lived, as he was soon rounded up by Kit Carson and sent on the Long Walk. In captivity at Fort Sumner, Atsìdì Sanì's career came to a complete halt. It wasn't until he was released with the rest of the Navahos that he began to practice his craft and teach it to others, beginning the era when silversmithing would become an "Indian Art."

Until 1880, all of the jewelry made by Indians was made for personal adornment. After 1880, the traders began to buy the silver ornaments and resell them to non-Indians. In 1890, Hermann Schweizer, working for the Fred Harvey Company, began making arrangements for Indian silversmiths to produce jewelry for the tourist trade. Working through the Thoreau Trading Post, Schweizer passed silver and gemstones to the silversmiths, who returned finished pieces of jewelry. These smiths worked at home and at first were given complete artistic license. Soon, the Fred Harvey Company discovered what the tourists would buy and began to order jewelry to suit tourist tastes.

The requirements for tourist jewelry were several. It must be lighter than the jewelry made by the Indians for themselves because it was thought that the tourists would not like heavy things. The jewelry was to be set with tourmalines instead of turquoise because turquoise was considered to be "too dear." Finally, the jewelry must look "Indian" because that was what was expected.

To this end, the traders and the Fred Harvey contractors began furnishing the Navaho silversmiths with metal design stamps. These stamps were used to make borders and other designs on the tourist jewelry. The stamps were designed by Anglos according to what they thought "looked Indian." In this way, arrows, swastikas, stick horses, lightning bolts, rainclouds, thunderbirds, and bear pawprints found their way onto "Indian Jewelry." A genre or a tradition was established that was not directly connected to the artisans who produced it.

When you reach exit 26 along Interstate 40, you will have to make some choices. This exit is the one to take if you want to enter Gallup on Route 66. This is also the exit to choose if you want to visit Red Rock State Park and Mr. Wilson's trading post.

RED ROCK STATE PARK

This New Mexico state park nestles against the base of the red, red cliffs that form the entire northern horizon. Once you see these cliffs, you will agree that no other name would have been appropriate. At Red Rock State Park you can picnic or camp overnight. There are recreational vehicle areas and restrooms equipped with hot showers. Besides the camping and picnicking facilities, Red Rock State Park also has a rodeo arena, exhibit halls, a visitors center, and a trading post. The Intertribal Indian Ceremonial (see p. 130) is held here every year in addition to assorted hot air balloon fiestas, fairs, and rodeos. Few sights are as awe-inspiring as a zillion cars and trucks heading to Red Rock State Park for the ceremonial, or as confusing and beautiful as seeing a jewel-hued hot air balloon rising against these red cliffs. Red Rock State Park is definitely a place where the unusual can occur.

Red Rock Trading Post, or Mr. Wilson's, as it was familiarly known, is backed up against the red cliffs, to the east of the park entrance. You can't actually see the place until you are very close to it because it is hidden deeply in a great grove of trees. To get there, pick out the biggest mass of greenery east of Red Rock State Park and at the base of the cliffs. Head off in that direction, following any of the little roads going that way. You may think that these are skimpy directions, but you really can't miss it and you really can't get lost. (Don't laugh, just drive.)

Mr. Wilson's, which is quite different from the tourist trap trading posts along Route 66, has been designated a historical New Mexico landmark and, in fact, history was actually made here. Mr. Wilson's was a cool and quiet store, a trading company in the purest sense. Mr. Wilson was a friend of the Navaho, a man truly interested in seeing them prosper and coexist with the Anglo world. One of his contributions to this ideal was to encourage a small revolution in the Navaho wool industry.

For many years Navaho shepherds and wool growers had sheared their sheep, bundled the wool they wanted to sell into a bag, and sold it by the pound at their local trading post. Prices for wool from Navaho sheep were always lower than prices for wool from other sources. This was not a reflection on the quality of the Navaho wool but a result of its packaging. Wool buyers knew that the Navaho wool was not sorted and that they would have to spend time and money separating the short wool clipped from the sheeps' legs from the long wool clipped from the back. The Navahos had always been aware of the difference in quality between the long and short wool clippings, and Navaho weavers had sorted their own wool because the longer fibers were easier to spin and made stronger yarn for weaving. But neither the wool growers nor the traders had ever discussed changing the wool trading practices of the past decades. Under Wilson's encouragement, the Navahos in this area began to separate the wool for sale by quality and length. Wilson was then able to get a better price for the wool, which he passed along to the wool growers. A new way of dealing with the wool gradually evolved.

Mr. Wilson was also ahead of his time in another area. When the Hollywood movie companies came to Gallup to film Western movies against the red cliffs, he had an idea. The Navahos needed work. Why not let the Indians play the Indians in the movies? Why should the movie companies hire Anglos as extras and make them up to look like Indians? Acting as a go-between for the Indians and the movie companies, Mr. Wilson helped the Navahos get work in the film industry.

"I remember meeting Mr. Wilson. He was a little, fat, friendly man. He had the enviable position among the Anglos of being a man who could get along with the Navahos. Among the Navahos he was known as a man who understood the Anglos. He wore Mexican-toed cowboy boots and the toes of his boots turned right up. He had a sloppy Stetson and a moderate-sized silver-and-turquoise belt buckle. His shirt stuck out around the top of his pants because of his round belly. He was one of the few people I ever met who didn't think of the Navahos as Indians but rather as ordinary people. They were his customers and he was a businessman. He really liked them. There was something about his demeanor, about his way with both Navaho and Anglo that was different from most of the people I ever met in Gallup. It was sure an eye-opener to hear that little fat man rattle away in Navaho. He was very light complected. He just didn't look like someone who would speak Navaho.

One day I had some time to kill in Gallup and I went out to the movie sets to see how they made movies. It was a God-awful hot day out there on the desert and they were filming some kind of massacre scene between the Good Guys and the Indians. The assistant director had those people go through the scene about four times and there was a lot of dust and horses and gunfire and arrows. It looked like hard work and nothing glamorous at all.

When everyone stopped for a break, I spotted a man I knew, an Indian from Tolani Lake, and I went over to speak to him. I asked him how he liked dying four times a day for eight dollars. He was an older man and it seemed like a lot of physical exertion to be riding a horse full tilt and then fall off and hit the dirt hard and lay there while the rest of the cast thundered on by. He got real quiet and his eyes got sort of hard. It was almost a full minute before he answered, 'Hell, I've died a hundred times for nothing, just trying to get a clerk to wait on me, in Gallup.' "

In the late thirties and throughout the forties, fifties, and sixties, the Hollywood film industry was in love with this part of New Mexico. If you were one of those children who spent every Saturday morning at the movies, you might recognize the scenery around Gallup. Countless Good Guys and Bad Guys chased each other across this section of the desert in front of these red cliffs while the cameras rolled. And in the evenings, the famous, the near-famous, and the struggling-to-be-famous would remove their make-up and retire to Gallup.

GALLUP TO
THE ARIZONA BORDER

GALLUP

Gallup, New Mexico is like a border town. It is a place where cultures come together and clash. It shares a margin with the Navaho Reservation. It is close to the home of the Zuni Indians. In the early 1880s it was the pay station for the workers on the Atlantic and Pacific Railroad; when payday came, everyone went to see the paymaster, David Gallup. The town that would bear his name was also the supply center and railhead for the Gallup American Coal Company, better known as Gamerco. And Gallup was one of the big stops for travelers on Route 66.

In Gallup there have always been the permanent residents who called the town home, but there have been plenty of others: the shifting, changing population who came to Gallup for supplies, information, or jobs and then left. Gallup was not a "planned community"; it grew as necessity required, expanding to take care of a highly mobile and transient population. Many of the businesses in Gallup were started for this reason and as a result Gallup has been called a community of merchants. Although the coal company closed the mines and the railroad is no longer the vibrant pulse of the United States, travelers are still arriving in Gallup looking for a meal, a night's lodging, or life's necessities. Although the freeway detours around Gallup instead of taking you through the heart of the city, like Route 66 did, the merchants in Gallup are still waiting on and catering to the traveler.

Get off the Interstate at exit 26. You are now on the original route of old 66. You can enter Gallup and see it just as many travelers did in the past. As you drive through Gallup along the main drag, you will be travelling parallel to the railroad tracks. Although Gallup has grown, changed, and modernized with fast-food restaurants, gas stations, motels, curio shops, tourist traps, and shopping centers, the old railroad tracks are never far away.

Trains bought supplies and goods to the Gallup merchants, and travelers and tourists to the Southwest. Trains carried away the coal, cattle, sheep, and wool. Trains sustained the Gallup economy. Even now, no matter where you choose to spend the night, you will probably wake to hear the trains rush and whistle through the dark. That's Gallup.

Being a culture-lap town, Gallup has some problems with its image. The media are often quick to make news of drunkenness, crime, and human misery, but one Gallup lady is tirelessly leading a campaign to overcome whatever problems her town has. She works continually to present the interesting aspects of Gallup's colorful history to the world and to reveal to the travelers the many beautiful tourist attractions that Gallup has to offer. This lady is Judi Snow, head of the Gallup Convention Center and Visitors' Bureau. When you visit Gallup, be sure to visit her at the Gallup Travel Center.

In the old days of Route 66, Gallup used to begin at Earl's Restaurant. Located on the north side of Route 66, Earl's was the first sure sign that you had really hit town. Earl's is still open in Gallup and it's still in the same place, but now you must drive *through* a considerable chunk of Gallup before you finally reach it. If you are hungry, stop and have a meal here. Earl's serves basic American restaurant food; it is hot, wholesome, and exactly what a traveler requires—roadside diner food that satisfies your hunger so you can get on down the road. Earl's opens early for breakfast, too!

Gallup has been called the Indian Capital of the World. There are many Indians in Gallup, near Gallup, around Gallup. There are Indian schools, hospitals, and agencies in Gallup. The government agencies connected to the Native American populations are among the biggest employers in the area. Indians are a big part of the business of Gallup.

For a long time, Indians were not accepted in Gallup. They couldn't buy a drink and some restaurants and stores would not serve them. In the words of the Peddler, it was tough being an Indian in Gallup. Most of that has changed now. People are more aware of the Native American contributions to the United States. Times change, minds change.

[A note from the author and photographer: there are people who read this book in manuscript and warned us that it was biased in favor of Native Americans. We agree wholeheartedly.]

THE EL RANCHO HOTEL

Just beyond Earl's, start looking for a green patch of grass surrounded by a split rail fence. Look for a sign that says "The El Rancho Hotel." You should be able to spot the long, low buildings on the left side of the road. If you like the past, nostalgia, and romance, spend a night at the El Rancho.

In former years, the El Rancho Hotel was one of the premier hotels in the Southwest. Built in 1937 by the brother of a Hollywood movie mogul, it was an outpost of elegance in a remote setting, elegant yet rugged, like an old-time cattle baron. For fifty years the El Rancho graced the side of Route 66. Toward the end, it passed through a series of owners and went into a slow decline. It was sad to see the once-glorious showplace slowly dying. The final indignity, before the doors closed in 1987, was the parking lot auction. All the fine furnishings that made the El Rancho the unique and comfortable inn that it was were hauled into the parking lot and auctioned off. It was sad, like a great lady selling her gowns for grocery money.

Today the doors of the El Rancho are open once again. Cars fill the parking lot and tourists check in to the rooms for an overnight stop in Gallup. The lobby looks welcoming, and on cooler days a fire crackles in the great stone fireplace. Armand Ortega, the new owner, tried to trace and reacquire the original furnishings of the old hotel. He re-created the visual impact of the old El Rancho even if he could not replace the old touches that made this a one-of-a-kind place.

In its heyday, for example, the El Rancho featured a brick-floored lobby that was two stories high under rough-cut beams. The massive supporting pillars and beams were hung with Navaho rugs, trophy deer heads, and other assorted wildlife souvenirs from hunting trips of the past. In fact, the El Rancho gave the impression of an exclusive hunting lodge. A huge stone fireplace nestled between the two curving, rustic staircases that led up to the mezzanine overlooking the lobby.

The old El Rancho Hotel, circa 1950.

In those days the El Rancho didn't just look luxurious, it was luxurious. You could dine in the dining room, breakfast in the coffee shop, and drink and dance in the bar. It had a full-service beauty parlor, a barber shop, and maid service. You could find a shoeshine boy, a newsboy, or bellboys and waitresses by the score.

When Route 66 went past the El Rancho, you stayed there if you could afford it. It was an experience to look forward to, an experience to remember. In the early days of the El Rancho, when the lawn in front was wide and green and the highway in front was narrow and quiet, it cost only a few dollars to spend the night in luxury and comfort. Ah, those were the days, my friend.

"In the forties and the fifties, the El Rancho was *the* place to stay in Gallup. Of course, all of the peddlers, all of the traveling salesmen wanted to stay in the best places. Selling and traveling was hard work, or so we thought, and so we always stayed in the best places we could. All of the peddlers tended to stay at the same places, anyway. We all had the same customers and the same basic routes up and down 66. The choice of where to stay at the end of the day was sometimes limited. There weren't that many places to sleep or eat or drink in many of those small towns, anyway. In Gallup, you stayed at the El Rancho, you drank and danced at the El Corral across the street, and you gambled . . . well, I'm not going to say where that went on. Too many people still alive, too many cops. Hell, they may still be playing cards in those places."

The gentility and luxury of the El Rancho attracted others, besides the tourists and the traveling salesmen. The fine old hotel was the headquarters of the Hollywood stars and the movie companies that came to Gallup between the early forties and the late sixties, when dozens of movies were filmed in this part of New Mexico. All the actors and actresses left an autographed picture of themselves at the El Rancho, and the pictures were hung in the bar and lobby: William

Bendix, Kirk Douglas, Rosalind Russell, Humphrey Bogart, Jay Silver-heels, all of them left a photographic memento at the El Rancho. Even the young, unknown B actors left their publicity stills. Ronald Reagan's photograph was one among the hundreds of pictures in the El Rancho's gallery.

Today, some of these autographed photos are hanging in the mezzanine gallery of the El Rancho. Many others are on the walls of a Gallup beauty salon, their new owner the high bidder at the parking lot auction.

"You know Gallup was not a cultural town during those times. It was a small town, a movie town, a business town. I remember so clearly how exciting it was when those movie people would come to Gallup. These people were famous. Everyone had seen them in the movies. They were familiar yet they were special, different. You could go into the lobby of the El Rancho and it would be full of those Hollywood people. They would be laughing and talking and planning things. They would talk to you, talk to anyone. The world was a different place, then. Those people could go on being people while they were in Gallup. They didn't need bodyguards to protect them from crowds. If you met them at the El Rancho they would talk to you, drink with you, dance with you. All kinds of people stayed at the El Rancho. Alan Ladd was there, once, making *Shane*. Robert Montgomery and Kirk Douglas stayed there, too. Everyone stayed at the El Rancho and you could find their photographs on the walls, in the lobby or the bar, after they were gone."

Summers in Gallup are hot. Winters are cold. The management of the El Rancho tried to bring comfort to their guests by using louvered doors on all the main-floor guest rooms, apparently to promote the circulation of both hot and cold air, depending on the season. It had the side effect of allowing the guests who were walking through the halls the odd opportunity of hearing fragments of what was being said in the rooms. A trip from your room to the bar might let you hear something like this as you went along:

"Do you think Muggsy will be all right out in the car?"
"If you didn't want to play, why did you come?"
"Must be at least 80 degrees!"
"Yes, I'll always love you!"
"Did you see that woman in the . . . ?"
"OOH! OOH! You're hurting my neck!"
"Yes, I'm the one who folded up the !@#$%¢&* + map that way!"
Although the Old El Rancho is gone, the restored El Rancho is alive

FINE
FOODS

STEAKS

CHICKEN
IN
BASKET

SHRIMP

AND

SAND-
WICHES

MIXED

DRINKS

YOU ARE

ASSURED

AN

EVENING

OF

FUN

DANCING NIGHTLY TO THE MUSIC OF
BUSTER AND HIS TRIO

LEFT TO RIGHT
NORMAN BUSTER, HERBERT HAANAHS, AND
NORMAN EBRON

Mary Sweany   Your Hostess

EL CORRAL

EAST 66 AVE.   PHONE 286-W

Music and dancing were the real attractions of the El Corral. Newspaper ad from the January 24, 1952 issue of the McKinley County Warrior.

and well. It is pleasurable to check in for a short visit to the recent past. The coffee shop is open and so is the bar. There are fewer Hollywood stars in the lobby but the management has replaced the room numbers with names of those famous actors and actresses so their presence is not forgotten. The Lone Ranger and Tonto actually did sleep here.

THE EL CORRAL

Across the street from the El Rancho was the El Corral. The El Corral was a special bar that could have been considered just a honky-tonk by some, but the glamour and elegance of the El Rancho, with its exotic, glittering guests, somehow rubbed off on the El Corral. The El Corral had a twenty-foot bar, dim lights, and a hardwood dance floor.

"I always went to the El Corral when I was in Gallup. You could get a good quiet meal at the Harvey House by the depot or you could get a steak at the El Rancho and then you could go to the El Corral for the rest of the evening. They always had good music at the El Corral. Sometimes it was a local band and sometimes it was a band from out of town. A band from Los Angeles might be traveling through, might have gotten off the train to spend a night in Gallup and they might be playing at the El Corral. Sometimes there were advertisements all over town about the music at the El Corral and sometimes, if it was a group passing through that the management just got for the night, you could hear about it from the bellhops or the waitresses or the men in the barbershops. Gallup had a pretty good communication system for things like that.

I remember a railroad man named Kid Cummings. He used to be a regular at the El Corral. He got off of those trains at the end of his work day, he got cleaned up, and he would go dancing at the El Corral. He was a dude, a dandy. He always wore spats. Ever see a man with spats? Kid Cummings was never without them. He used to take one of the Gallup schoolteachers to the El Corral. We called them old maid schoolteachers in those days but I guess that's not modern now. Guess she was just an unmarried lady who taught school. Her name was Barnett. She might have had a first name, she must have had one but everyone just called her Barnett. Kid Cummings and Barnett . . . those two could dance! They were practically a floorshow all by themselves. It was wonderful to see two people enjoy themselves so much. They were a part of the El Corral.

The movie stars used to come to the El Corral, too. Nothing was exclusive in Gallup. If you wanted to drink and dance you went to the El Corral. Everyone went there. Used to see that Indian who played Tonto, there. He was a big man. I got the idea that he was a tough man, a mean man. Maybe I was wrong. I thought at the time that that big man hated me, hated everyone. Still, it couldn't have been easy being an Indian in Hollywood. Hollywood wasn't too enlightened, then. And it damn sure wasn't easy being an Indian in Gallup. Maybe that man had reason to be tough.

If you didn't like the El Corral, you could go downtown and there would be excitement there, too. The coal miners would come to town and they would always have just wads and wads of money. They usually went downtown for their drinking and fun. The bars were a little rougher and for some reason, most of them were downstairs, below the street. You had to walk down a flight of stairs to enter them. Maybe the miners felt at home in those dim, basement bars. The

White Elephant was the one I remember the plainest. The miners would sit in the smoky light and tell the most wonderful stories, all lies, about their dangerous exploits. It was something to hear them. They worked in another world. I guess they did have a dangerous life. When they came to Gallup, they really did unwind. They spent money, time, and booze like no one I ever saw. They were men apart."

NATIVE AMERICAN ART

One of the most widely recognized contributions of the Native Americans has been their unique art. At one time, Indian-made jewelry, baskets, rugs, paintings, pottery, and beadwork were regarded as either cheap tourist junk or a specialized art form admired only by anthropologists and specialist art collectors. Today, this is not the case. Native American art is sought after and admired all over the world. Three events coincided to create this new viewpoint and the resulting demand for Native American art. First, in the early 70s, *The Wall Street Journal* printed a front-page article describing Native American art and artifacts as one of the soundest investments possible. Second, there was a renewed interest in primitive art. Third, the Southwest became the focus of trendy fashion ranging from food and interior design to clothes, shoes, and jewelry. Although some of the excitement about the Southwest is bound to fade, the value of Native American art is now firmly established.

In Gallup you can find an extraordinary variety of Native American weaving, pottery, baskets, and jewelry. Some art galleries exhibit only paintings by Native American artists, and certain shops show only Native American jewelry. In the small world of Native American art, patrons and customers alike drop the names of prominent silversmiths, painters, and weavers. It is a sophisticated world. It is no longer a world where a trader exchanged the necessities of life for a blanket or a piece of silver-and-turquoise jewelry.

Much of the art you will find in Gallup is made by local artists. Some shops deal in a vast variety of art, however, and the owners of these stores may "import" Native American work from other states and other groups of Native Americans not indigenous to New Mexico or the Southwest. If you get the urge to purchase Native American crafts in Gallup, use your common sense. If you see something you like, you should probably buy it and enjoy it. If it is important to you that you own something Authentic, Meaningful, Valuable, Artistic, and Evocative, then take your time. Either read everything you can about the craft you are interested in before you come to Gallup or be prepared to spend hours listening to other people in Gallup give you their opinions, interpretations, and points of view about Indian art. Although many of the people you might meet in the Gallup art market will be well educated, well informed and well established, do not expect many of the dealers to be Native Americans.

SILVER JEWELRY AND THE PAWN SYSTEM

If you are interested in Native American jewelry, Gallup is a great place to shop for it. The Zunis, the Navahos, and the Hopis all market their jewelry there. A very rough, very general rule of thumb for distinguishing the maker of the jewelry you find is this: Zuni jewelry is often delicate, with many tiny, cut turquoise stones. Navajo jewelry is usually more massive, using several large turquoise in each piece or plain silver with no stones. Some Hopi work is called overlay, characterized by a design or silhouette cut from one piece of silver and laid over another that has been blackened.

The two types of jewelry to shop for are modern and pawn. Modern jewelry is made by the silversmith specifically for sale. It is intended for the market and must be marked "sterling" if it is silver and "Indian made" if it is Indian made. Approach this last label with a consumer's awareness. "Indian made" does not necessarily mean made by hand. Jewelry marked "Indian made" might easily be jewelry that is mass produced, made by machines operated by Native Americans. According to the law, that's "Indian made."

"Pawn" or "old pawn" or "dead pawn" is the other type of jewelry to shop for. These items were usually made by the silversmith for himself, his family, or a friend, and not originally intended for the mass market. It is often heavier, of higher quality, older and more valuable than modern pieces of jewelry and as a result is rare and expensive.

In the not-too-distant past, this type of jewelry was an integral part of a well-established Southwestern economic system between the traders and the Indians. The Indians invested their wealth in silver and turquoise, which was portable, accessible, and its value was well recognized. When the Indian wanted or needed either cash or supplies, he would pawn a piece of jewelry to the trader. Both parties in the transaction clearly understood that the piece of jewelry would be redeemed, and until that time the trader would guard it carefully and keep it safe. When the harvest was in, the sheep sold, the check arrived, or a more prosperous time of year was underway, the Indian would return to the trading post and buy back the pawned jewelry.

This was a functional credit system. Some traders report that they had the same pieces of jewelry pawned to them over and over for twenty or thirty years, essentially the adult lifetime of the owner. A fair pawn system created much goodwill at a trading company. The trader was assured that his customers would be coming back. The customers were confident that their wealth was safe in the trader's vault or even on display in the pawn case. There was no social stigma associated with this pawn system as there sometimes is with the pawn shop system in the Anglo world.

Naturally, life being as uncertain as it is, some pieces of jewelry were never claimed because the owners died, went away, or became permanently impoverished, and these pieces were eventually sold. It cannot be emphasized too strongly that a trader with a working pawn system would never sell a piece of jewelry pawned to him as long as his other customers, the rest of his community, had faith that the original owner could someday redeem it. This part of the system had nothing to do with any legislated rules about pawnbroking, and everything to do with the essential trust and confidence that the system was based on. (This is not to say that a little exploitation did not work on both sides of the system. It was a human system, after all.)

Go and visit an established trader in Gallup. Look in his "old pawn" case and see the quality and variety of jewelry there. Compare it to the pieces for sale in the rest of his display cases. It is fascinating to see the differences in design and materials over time. The jewelry of the twenties, thirties, forties, and fifties is completely different from that of the most recent decades.

RICHARDSON'S

A good place to start an exploratory shopping trip might be Richardson's. This unpretentious establishment, which has been in Gallup for many years, is across the street from the railroad station, right on Route 66. The entrance to Richardson's looks small and modest and completely belies the extensive rooms within. In spite of its unlikely appearance and location, it is worth a visit. It is one spot in Gallup where you could see and learn any number of things.

While stopping in this neighborhood, you might do some window shopping and walking. Downtown Gallup is just a couple of blocks to the south. Other pawn shops, cafes, rescue missions, and gift shops are in this area, which is not the regular tourist beat but is nonetheless interesting and informative.

A few doors down from Richardson's you will find a shop selling beautifully ornamented, two-and-a-half-gallon water buckets. These buckets, along with the feather fans and gourd rattles that are also sold here, are used in the ceremonies of the Native American Church, a nationwide religious sect that is a unique blend of Christianity and traditional Native American religious ideals. It made its appearance among the Native Americans of this country just before the turn of the century. Although this religion has a long history of opposition from traditionalists in both cultures, it seems to be a positive force that has helped many Native Americans to live successfully in both the Anglo and the Indian world. Aside from the fact that it is not the traditional religion of the people of the Southwest, the primary objection to this church is its use of peyote in highly ritualized and formal ceremonies. The use of peyote as a religious sacrament is completely legal. This is not drug abuse.

The symbol most commonly associated with the Native American Church is the waterbird. It looks like a stylized Christian dove. The waterbird can be found on hatpins, lapel pins, earrings, and watchbands, or you may see it in paintings, on pottery, and in beadwork. Like every other symbol, its meaning and value depends on individual experience and interpretation.

THE THUNDERBIRD

If you are interested in the beginnings of things, if you like to see the guts of an industry, if like tools or raw materials, then you might want to go and visit the Thunderbird Jewelry Supply house on the west side of Gallup. Drive west on Route 66 until you spot the store on the south or left side of the road. It has a very large sign out in front that says "Thunderbird Jewelry Supply." There is also a Thunderbird Jewelry Store nearby so be sure of which one you want to visit.

As you enter the store through the big glass front doors, the first thing you will notice is the smell of popcorn. The Thunderbird people have popcorn here to nourish their customers, entertain the customers' children while their parents shop, and because some people just plain like popcorn. This is the place where handmade jewelry begins. This is one of the places where silversmiths buy sheets of sterling silver, coils of sterling silver wire, and such semiprecious stones as turquoise, coral, jet, malachite, and lapis lazuli. This is the place where an artist who works with metal and stones can buy tools, chemicals, machinery, polishing compounds, and everything else that it will take to bring an idea into three-dimensional form.

Browse through the cases. Look at the merchandise. Seeing the elemental stuff of jewelry, seeing the cost of the materials helps explain why art objects cost what they do. It gives an idea of the great transformation that occurs when an artist begins with a flat sheet of silver and turns it into a beautiful silver bracelet. After a visit to the Thunderbird, all a person needs to create a work of art is time, skill, and an idea.

TRUCKS, TRUCKS, AND MORE TRUCKS

As you drive around Gallup you will eventually notice that many of the other vehicles on the street are trucks. The General Motors dealership in this town was once known as the largest truck dealer in the United States. More trucks were sold from Gallup than any other city.

A great many of the truck-buyers are Navahos, and some of the truck dealers will accept a steer or a hand-woven rug instead of money for a truck payment. Trucks make sense if you live on the reservation. Once you leave Gallup and drive out into the countryside, out into the Navaho reservation, you will understand. The country of the reservation (young people call it the "Res") is very rugged and sparsely populated. People live far apart. Most of them must haul wood and water for their day-to-day needs. Many of the roads are dirt and ruts. Some new truck buyers live so far away from Gallup and drive their trucks so much that they can return to town for the 10,000-mile check-up just six weeks after leaving the showroom.

THE GALLUP INTERTRIBAL CEREMONIAL

If you plan to be traveling down Route 66 in the late summer, you may want to visit Gallup during the Intertribal Ceremonial, when Indians from all over North America gather for a gigantic fair. Everyone is invited to attend and the attractions include rodeos, parades, beauty pageants, arts-and-crafts competitions and sales, dance competitions or pow-wows, good food, lots of people, and a general good time.

This event is held at Red Rock State Park (see p. 115) and is sponsored in part by the merchants and the Chamber of Commerce of Gallup. It is a memorable experience. Unless you are a completely jaded citizen of the world, you are bound to see something beautiful, surprising, or completely new. The Intertribal Ceremonial has a hundred facets, not the least of which is that it is a gathering of wonderful, complex, and endlessly intriguing human beings.

"The Gallup Ceremonial used to be much smaller. The Red Rock Park didn't exist when I first attended. The ceremonial was held on the north side of town. Hundreds of Navahos and their friends would come to Gallup, many of them riding in their high wagons pulled by teams, and they would camp in the rocks and along the cliffs on the far side of the railroad tracks. The merchants of Gallup would organize contests and sponsor prizes for the winners. Some of those contests had a lot of imagination going for them. I remember there was a fire-building contest for the ladies and footraces for the little kids. The men all brought their wildest horses for the rodeo and their fastest ones for the horse-race. There was even a bareback race for the Navaho matrons. Different tribes presented different dances in the evening. There were men who could do fancy rope tricks and all kinds of displays of skill. There were contests for the best rug woven and the most beautiful jewelry made by the most skillful silversmith. The Gallup merchants would do a lot of buying during the ceremonial and of course they made money, too.

The people dressed up. Everyone tried to wear the newest clothes they could and all of their jewelry. Even the housewives of Gallup would put on all of their Indian jewelry and their long fiesta skirts.

It was like a county fair at the same time. People showed their fattest sheep and their best wool producers. There was always someone from the Health Department and the BIA to tell about sanitation and education. There was cotton candy and popcorn and fry bread and other good things to eat.

At night you could look out onto the hills and see hundreds of tiny fires where the Indians were camping outside of the city. If you went closer and walked in the darkness you could hear the soft monotonous chanting of the people singing. It drifted on the air like piñon smoke and although you couldn't understand the words, it was real soothing. It was beautiful to be out under the stars in the darkness and hear that low rhythm and feel all of the people around you, yet scattered out, in Gallup and at the little fires. Even the sound of the trains going by didn't seem to interfere.

I remember one ceremonial I became real disturbed. I had been standing in downtown Gallup watching the parade. They always had a big parade for the ceremonial and the Indians would turn out in their silver jewelry and velvet clothes. The Zunis would come, too. They always had what they called the 'olla maidens,' walking in the parade. The olla maidens were Zuni ladies, all heavily swathed in priceless silver, and shell-and-turquoise jewelry. They wore black dresses and white wrappings on their legs and each one of them walked with a large pot or *olla* balanced on her head. The streets of Gallup are really hilly after you turn off of 66 and the ladies would stride majestically up and down the hilly streets and their pots never tumbled. I never even *heard* of an olla maiden losing her pot! There were young olla maidens of seven or so and older olla maidens of eighty or more and every age in between. These ladies just embodied dignity. Their carriage would put a duchess to shame and they walked about two miles.

The Navahos would ride in the parade, too. Whole families would pile into their wagons and the horses would be curried and shining and there would always be some silver on their harnesses and headstalls, too. The wagons would slide down those hills in Gallup with the brakes locked and the people riding in them would laugh and shout and have an exciting time. The Navahos aren't really solemn people.

There were marching bands from the high schools and veterans and Boy Scouts but mostly there were Indians. Mostly there were Indians and they paraded right through downtown Gallup, past the shops and the restaurants with the signs in the windows that read, 'No Indians Allowed.'

That year was the first time I ever really saw those signs. They really bothered me. I couldn't sleep so I walked out into the darkness and I heard some singing and I just sat down on the ground and listened. I sat there all night. Sometimes that kind of singing is connected to some kind of healing ceremony or medicine, not a good time like the ceremonial. I couldn't tell where the singing was coming from but I just sat in the darkness, listening. Maybe it was some kind of medicine. When the singing ended, just before dawn, I felt better. Those damn signs were still in the windows but I felt calmer. I walked back to the hotel and slept a few hours. I haad to get on down the road. I had calls to make.

Times change. When I was a young man in Gallup it was so much fun to stop and drink and dance. I remember my first snow was in Gallup, too. I was raised in the South and had never seen any snow until one morning I woke up in the El Rancho, looked out of the window and saw six inches of new snow. I decided immediately that I was snowbound forever. I had literally never seen snow before.

I used to like to walk the streets of Gallup. I liked to see the Indians in their velvet and their silver and turquoise. In those days the ladies always walked about two steps behind the men. That was funny because the women were usually the rulers in the family. Those Indians, those people, theirs was truly a barbaric splendor. To me they were visitors from another world. I didn't think I could ever visit their world; it was too far away from mine.

Now I understand that these people are not Indians at all, but Native Americans. I've heard that they have all the same problems that we do, like drinking and drugs and theft and divorce and suicide. Things called 'social problems,' for heaven's sakes. Let's get out of here, kid. I just don't know how to think about it all."

To get out of Gallup, take Route 66 and head west.

GALLUP TO THE ARIZONA BORDER

It's only twenty-six miles from Gallup to the Arizona border. Getting onto Route 66 to head west takes a bit of maneuvering, but it's worth it. Don't get on the interstate. Drive west out of Gallup on Railroad Avenue—Route 66. Just outside of Gallup proper, look for a left-hand turn that will take you under I-40. Go through here, stop at the stop sign, and turn right. Very quickly, you will see that the country has shaken off the tawdry clothes of the city and the character of the land begins to appear. Glide past the truck-weighing station, turn right, and go under I-40 again. Turn left. Drive across the old bridge that is straight in front of you.

What a relief! You're back on Route 66 again. The railroad track is between you and the interstate. The Rio Puerco cuts a deep looping course through the land. (This is not the same Rio Puerco that is outside of Albuquerque. This Rio Puerco is correctly known as the Rio Puerco of the West, although few people in this area call it anything but the Rio Puerco. There are, in fact, three Rio Puercos in New Mexico; the third one is in Santa Fe County.) As you follow the river's lead, you can see weird formations of rock and eroded soil. Friendly, high bluffs and wide, wide vistas are the backdrop for homesites tucked up in each little canyon. There are chickens and dogs in the dooryards and basketball hoops on the barns.

Some things haven't changed. Although the Burma Shave Company took down all of its signs, other forms of roadside advertising persists. This stretch of road is peppered with signs advertising Fort Yellow Horse. The signs promise many splendid and amazing things, which is what the tourist and traveler is always looking for. Read the signs carefully. You are almost to the Arizona border. The huge cluster of buildings up ahead is Fort Yellow Horse. Route 66 snakes past them and heads into Arizona.

"I think those people at Fort Yellow Horse must be new in the business. I bet they don't last. They aren't advertising the most important things at a tourist trap. I didn't see a single sign that said 'Last Chance for Gas' or 'Get your waterbags here' or 'See Rattlesnakes Live!' Yep, I think those people are missing a bet!"

ALBUQUERQUE AGAIN

It was the end of the trip. The grey Packard was back in the garage and the Peddler and I were back in the lobby of the La Posada.

"It was a great trip," I said sincerely. "Thanks for sharing it with me."

"Oh hell, kid," the Peddler said, "I had fun. I loved all of those old places. Made me feel alive again to know they're still out there."

"We stood there, neither of us willing to shake hands and let old 66 fade away.

"I'll be back again soon," I said. "I'll need some help with my notes. You can read what I've written and let me know if it's right."

"Sure." The Peddler seemed to be stooping again. He looked a little smaller.

"I'll bring you copies of the book when I get it." I dragged out the moment, hating to go back and work at the typewriter, hating to be in an office instead of driving over the hills and beyond.

"OK, kid." The Peddler was not making any motions to leave, either.

"Is that everything then?" I asked.

"Guess so. Don't forget the part about the Longhorn Ranch, now. You know it wouldn't have been Route 66 without the Longhorn."

"The Longhorn! You never told me about that place. It's out to the east, isn't it? I went there when I was a kid. But it's gone now. They tore it down."

"Then I guess we'd better sit down and have a drink. I'll tell you all about it. You can't leave the Longhorn out." The Peddler's eyes were twinkling and he led the way to our regular chairs in the back of the lobby.

PART II

ALBUQUERQUE TO
THE TEXAS BORDER

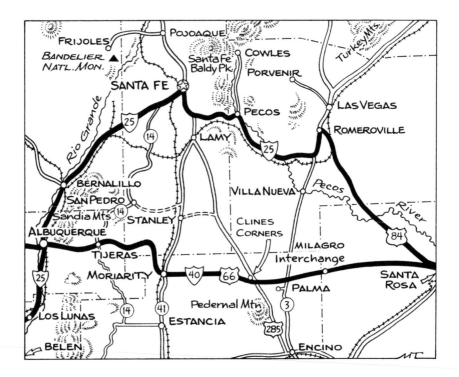

Map 5. *Albuquerque to Santa Rosa (based on* Roads to Cibola, *New Mexico State Highway Commission, 1929).*

ALBUQUERQUE
TO THE CANYON

WE HEAD EAST

The grey Packard had been washed and stood shining at the curb in front of the La Posada. The Peddler's grip and order book were on the back seat. I put my backpack beside them. As I slid into my place on the passenger's side, the Peddler let out the clutch and we eased around the corner to Third Street.

"What you have to remember about 66 to the east of Albuquerque," the Peddler said seriously, "is that it's not 66 to the west of Albuquerque. There aren't any Indian reservations or pueblos and so there aren't many Indians. There isn't any of that type of scenery that would bring a movie company out to make a movie so there aren't any movie stars. There are only a few startling geographic features along the road. Mostly you see just endless stretches of plains, mesas or *llanos*. Mostly it's just space. The big part of 66 to the east is the people and what they did, not the places."

The grey Packard turned left at Central Avenue and headed east. We were off again, traveling Route 66.

From Third Street and Central Avenue head east if you want to follow Route 66 through town to the mouth of Tijeras Canyon. The canyon is the gateway to the eastern section of New Mexico.

Central Avenue used to be the main street in Albuquerque but that changed as the city expanded and the businesses in the downtown area moved to industrial parks and high-rise offices in other parts of the town. Today Central Avenue is four, sometimes six lanes wide, decorated with landscaped dividers and four-eyed traffic lights. Only a few traces remain of the two-lane asphalt strip that carried the travelers in and out of the Duke City.

"There's the First National Bank Building, on the corner of Third and Central. I remember the time when every dentist and eye doctor in Albuquerque had an office in that building. There were regular M.D.'s in there, too. In those days, the bank only took up the first floor. I can't remember any lawyers in the bank building. It seems to me they all camped out in the Sunshine Building, down on the southeast corner of Second and Central. There were so many of them, even in those days, that many people called it 'The Lawyers' Building.'

Over to the right, where you can see the train station with the red roof, used to be the Alvarado Hotel. It was a beautiful old place, the biggest hotel owned by the Atchison, Topeka and Santa Fe Railroad. It had a big bar, an elegant restaurant and a gift shop for the tourists that was almost like a museum. It was a special place, a place to go when you wanted a special time.

The people who made the Alvarado their place were special, too. Gifford, of Gifford Taxi and Tours, was in the bar every night. He always wore a little black string tie like a frontier lawyer. Van Heflin the artist was a regular, there too. It was a different crowd from the Hilton. The Alvarado group was more colorful, more youthful, more arty. Sally Panich, the beautiful debutante, could be seen there every once in awhile, usually for dinner. And of course, Hugh Crooks was there when he was in town. Where did all of those people go?

I liked walking around that old hotel. It wasn't like the Old Hilton or the El Rancho. It was an elegant Fred Harvey establishment. There were big rooms with rich dark woods and elegant furnishings, there were wide, covered verandas that looked out over colorful flower beds. It was so cool and shady there on a hot day.

The train depot was built like the Alvarado Hotel with those shady, wide verandas. The Indians used to spread out their tourist stuff in the shade of those

"THE FAMOUS ALVARADO HOTEL, FIRST STREET & CENTRAL AVENUE. Known and remembered throughout the world by all who have stopped here. Famous for food, lodging, and entertainment and for hosting the patrons of the Santa Fe passenger trains."

verandas and sell it to the people as they got off the trains. That was one of things about those Fred Harvey places, there were always a few Indians around selling souvenirs to the tourists. It didn't matter if it was 1939 in Arizona or 1970 in Albuquerque, the Fred Harvey establishments were always glad to have the Indian vendors on their premises.

The old Alvarado is gone now. It was torn down in the seventies when the railroads were in decline. The owners said it cost too much to run the place, and no one cared. After they pulled it down, people started to holler. Said the city should have bought it. Said it was an irreplaceable landmark. Said it was progress! Bunch of bull! And too late, too."

As you drive on down Central, you leave the older part of Albuquerque behind. After you go under the railroad tracks and cross over Broadway, only a few signs of old Albuquerque, the dusty Route 66 town, are left; Albuquerque the big city is crowding out the past. From Broadway to the edge of town only occasional traces of the old highway remain. Here and there you can see an old tourist court with a Spanish name and a Southwest look to the architecture: the Aztec Lodge, the De Anza. Newer businesses along Central Avenue are now using the Highway 66 logo in their advertising, capitalizing on nostalgia and memory.

"Look at this place. It used to be that once you got to Monroe Street there was nothing here between you and the mountains but the State Fair Grounds, a few tourists places, and the Blue Spruce Lounge. The street didn't even have a curb and gutter. You could see sheep pens and windmills and empty, empty mesa. You could even see an antelope sometimes. Now I bet there isn't even a prairie dog.

In those days, when you drove down Central and got closer to the mouth of the canyon, and looked over to the right, the south, you could see the airplane graveyard. I guess that's about where Eubank Boulevard is now. After World War II there was a two-mile stretch of desert out there covered with old B-26s, B-24s, B-25s, and P-38s. As those planes weren't needed, they just flew them out here and parked them in the desert. A sad end for those old warplanes, but what can you do with so many bombers in peacetime?"

Keep driving on Central until you reach the Tramway Boulevard intersection. If you want to head east to the Texas border, get on Interstate 40 here and take off. It's about 200 miles to the state line and the highway is smooth and fast.

If you want to go east following the exact same path of Route 66, you can't do it. You just can't drive the old way because the road isn't there any more. The Interstate covers part of old 66, part of it is frontage road, and part of it is gone. However, if you use the following instructions, you can at least get an impression of what the Route 66 traveler saw before the highway engineers began to improve the road and built Interstate 40.

Start at the jambled intersection of Central and Tramway, bear right, and get on the road marked New Mexico 333. Almost immediately you will be in Tijeras Canyon. *Tijeras* means "scissors" in Spanish, and although some people say they can see the canyons forming an outline of scissors, Tijeras is also the name of the family that settled here in the mid 1880s.

Eight tenths of a mile from the intersection look to your right and spot the ruins of Little Beaver Town. This was an amusement park based on the cartoon strip, "Red Ryder and Little Beaver." Little Beaver Town was enclosed in a log palisade and looked very much like an old cavalry fort from the Western movies. Fred Harman, who drew the cartoon story, had his studio here.

Four tenths of a mile beyond Little Beaver Town, look down to your right and see the riding and boarding stable. When Route 66 was the road through the canyon, this was a country-western nightclub, a honky-tonk. A local TV celebrity, Dick Bills, was often the singer with star billing here. Dick Bills had his own band and when they played "When My Blue Moon Turns to Gold Again," he would sometimes ask his young nephew, Glenn Campbell, to sit in with the band and sing that song.

Drive a bit slowly now and take the road that directs you to "Albuquerque, West." This road will climb up out of the canyon and over the freeway. Once you are across the interstate, DO NOT TURN LEFT and go back to Albuquerque. Instead look to your right, spot the four lanes heading east and go "that-away." This was a section of Route 66. You can cruise a bit slowly here. This road does not have the hustle and urgency of the interstate. Glancing around, you can get the feeling of being enveloped in the mountains. Albuquerque is gone and who knows what lies ahead? This feeling was part of the 66 adventure.

When 66 was the main road through the canyon, the canyon dwellers were a smaller community. These days you can see houses, barns, and cars up every canyon and down every draw, but in the forties it wasn't like that. Each little building and house was the domain of an individual and news of them, characteristics of them, drifted with the travelers up and down 66.

"Echo Canyon, home of old Spider Webb. I remember that man. He had the most unusual tattoo, but it fit him just right. He had a spider tattooed on his left forearm, a red spider in a black web. It looked exactly like the neon sign hanging in front of his curio stand. He drew hundreds of tourists to his place with that flashing sign, it was a little unusual, a little macabre, but not threatening. And he had the prettiest jewelry in that shop. He got most of it from Mexico.

In the winters when there weren't any tourists, he relied on mail order. He used to write the ads himself and send them off to magazines. I remember sitting in a barbershop in Amarillo, Texas, reading a magazine and waiting for my turn. I started reading some of the ads in that magazine and really got caught up in one. It was an ad for some silver earrings shaped like hearts. The description was so exact, the idea was so interesting that I decided to buy some. Of course I was in love at the time and that influenced me. When I read the address where you were supposed to send the money, it was old Spider Webb in the canyon. I stopped on the way home and bought those earrings from Spider, himself.

Spider's neighbor was an elderly lady of about 60 who owned the Mountain Lodge. The place is still there but I'm sure the woman is gone now. I never knew her name but I was familiar with the story about her. Whenever the Mountain Lodge would come up in conversation, someone would be sure to say, 'Isn't that the place owned by that old lady who is a deer hunter? The one who can walk a half a mile from her back door and kill a deer? They say she gets one every year!' I never talked to that woman, never saw her but I could be in the Club Cafe in Santa Rosa, mention that I had driven through Tijeras Canyon, and some other roadrunner, another traveling salesman, would bring up the owner of the Mountain Lodge. It's funny what you become famous for. I wonder if that lady ever killed a deer, at all?"

Although Spider Webb's place is no longer open, you can still see the sign that says Echo Canyon. A little more than a mile beyond that the Mountain Lodge sits on the north side of the road. The canyon to the north where the lady owner was supposed to get her deer is now choked with houses and roads.

Swing your eyes around the high canyon walls. Midway up some of them you can glimpse a piece of old road hugging the side of the canyon. Some of these are sections of Route 66, while some are parts of the road that predated that highway. In Tijeras Canyon people talk about the old road, old 66, the old highway, and the interstate. There are at least four roads here and they are all old except Interstate 40.

Less than half a mile past the Mountain Lodge, the road will descend to an underpass, go under I-40 and swing into a sharp curve. This is the way Route 66 went and this infamous section of it was called Dead Man's Curve. Think of a dark night, an icy highway, and a tired driver in a big heavy Packard and you can figure out how the place got its name.

Driving along you are now close to the south side of the canyon. Interstate 40 should be to your left. When Route 66 went through Tijeras Canyon the motorists could look down on their right and see a little stream ruunning between the boulders and trees in the bottom of the canyon. The small creek is still purling through those rocks. It rises from the spot known as Seven Springs. When the old model T's used to boil and sputter from the high elevation and the steep road here, their drivers would nurse them along to Seven springs, where they could climb down to the springs and scoop up enough water to cool down the old Fords. There was a service station at Seven Springs and you can still see one of the buildings, paint-scarred and aging on the right side of the road. "Seven Springs" is still faintly visible on the face of this old survivor.

When you reach the interchange of New Mexico State Road 14 and Interstate 40, keep to your right and stay on 333. The Ideal Cement plant is on your right. The Ideal plant is different from many other cement plants. No heavy coating of cement dust clings to the trees and buildings around this facility. Built with precipitators to catch the flying dust, the Ideal plant was an early effort aimed at protecting the environment from the hazards of industry.

Continue driving down State Road 333. You should be between the village of Tijeras and the freeway. When you reach the fork in the road with the double signs that say Zamora Road, you have a choice. If you go to the left, you will be able to drive down a strip of Route 66. This is a dead-end jaunt and you will have to turn around and come back to the fork to travel on. If you don't wish to make this detour, keep to your right and drive on.

THE LITTLEST SIDE TRIP

Take the left fork at the double Zamora Road signs. This road is very short. It passes the Bernalillo County Sheriff Department's Substation, the Fire Department, and goes on to a dead end. At the end of the pavement, you might be greeted by some fierce-sounding and fierce-looking watchdogs. This is where you turn around. This road is not particularly scenic, historic, or exciting but the purist will have the satisfaction of actually being on an actual piece of old Route 66. As you drive back to the fork in the road, look again at the building that now houses the Sheriff's Department Substation. In the quieter days of Route 66 there used to be a diner here that specialized in pies.

"Sometimes driving was hard work. You had to pay attention, though. You had to drive; it took muscle and concentration. You couldn't just lay back on the upholstery and set the cruise control and go. You had to *drive*, you had to shift gears up and down all of these hills. Some days it was work. You could look out the window and see all of these pretty pine trees and white clouds or maybe spring flowers and you couldn't spend much time looking because the car and the road needed your attention. On days when you were tired of the work, you stopped often and ate a lot of pie and drank a lot of coffee. I liked to stop at that place along here where they specialized in pie. 'Pie' was written on the side of that cafe in letters about a foot high and next to that it said: 'Home Economist on the Premises.' It always seemed to me that if a home economist had made the pie it must be good for you. It couldn't possibly be fattening and you didn't need an excuse to eat a pie a Home Economist made. It was probably your duty."

Back on the road, stay to the right and keep traveling. The road will begin to rise and you will be able to see more than the steep canyon walls. Soon the land will open up and you can see a wide valley. You are closer to Interstate 40 now and you can hear the roar of the traffic on that hard grey snake. Eventually you will reach a point where an exit ramp road and New Mexico 333 converge. Turn left at the stop sign. Across the road you can see Caristo's Black Powder establishment. Head east. A small brown-and-white shield-shaped sign will tell you that once again you are following the path of Route 66.

TO MORIARTY

THE ROAD TO MORIARTY

Before you stretches a long straight shot of Route 66. Stay on it and you will reach Moriarty, New Mexico.

It is tranquil on this narrow road. To the north (left) you can still see and hear the flow and roar of the traffic on I-40. The noise is muted and the cars and trucks look small. On 66 you have time to gaze at the long valley reaching north and south on either side of the road. Hawks and ravens float through the air. The trill of meadowlarks drifts in through the open car windows. Gentle hills covered with piñon and juniper rise out of the plain. If it is late summer or early fall, purple asters and sunflowers will stand along the roadside.

Route 66 is not without the mark of man. The road does not go through an empty landscape. Mobile homes, small ranches, farms, wrecking yards, gas stations, housing developments, and real estate offices are scattered over the land. But there is space between. There is room in the wide landscape for everything.

Long rows of mailboxes, those symbols of civilization, stand at each intersection where dirt side roads meet the old two-lane blacktop. Their great number tells you about the population. You are approaching the village of Edgewood. On the edge of Edgewood, a large official-looking yellow sign proclaims the countryside a "Congested Area."

Edgewood was once a small village on the edge of Route 66, the community center for the dry-land farmers of this part of the valley. Now it is a larger village and many of the community members do not farm but commute to Albuquerque to work. The dry-land farmers are still growing wheat and beans in this long valley but new technology and irrigation systems are changing this pattern, also.

Edgewood is where a religious group known as the Blackstockings has its headquarters. Information about the Blackstockings is hard to come by. Except for the facts that these people are a sect of Christian fundamentalists and the women wear modest clothes and black stockings, I could never find out anything about this group. I never knew if there was nothing more to discover or if the people I asked didn't want to reveal what they knew. Some knowledge is not the business of a wanderer. If you are driving through Edgewood in late summer or early fall and see what looks like a sizeable community gathering, it is probably the Blackstockings' annual convention. If the ladies are all wearing black stockings and calf-length skirts you will know the Blackstockings are congregating.

In the past, when this highway was Route 66, a traveler would begin to see the famous (or infamous) cherry cider signs soon after driving through Edgewood. These signs announced that cool, delicious cherry cider was for sale on the top of Cherry Hill, two miles down the road.

"Cherry cider. I remember that stuff. On a hot day in a car without air conditioning, cool cherry cider sounded like such a tempting idea. On a hot day in a hot car filled with rowdy kids, cherry cider *was* an irresistible idea, especially if those kids could read the road signs.

The cherry cider stand was on the top of Cherry Hill. It was a small wooden stand, festooned with red bunting and pictures of red cherries and tall glasses of red cider. Somehow the artist managed to make the glasses in those simple pictures look frosty and inviting, made you long for some of that cool cherry cider, made you wonder what it would taste like. You had to wonder where the cherry trees were; there were none in sight.

When you pulled up at the stand, got out of your car, and got your money out, they served the stuff to you in a glass, not a paper cup. You had to stand there and drink it and give them back the glass. You got something that was cool, red, and sweet. It tasted suspiciously like red Kool Aid, but you were never sure: What was cherry cider suposed to taste like, anyway?"

Kline's Castle on old 66. "Castles are so impractical in the twentieth century."

Today there is a garage at the top of Cherry Hill. There are no pictures of cool glasses or bright red cherries. The stand with the bright bunting is gone. A small sign wired to the chain link surrounding the garage says "Cherry Hill." Drive past the Cherry Hill Garage and start looking to your left. Soon you will spot an equipment rental yard. Rising out of the herd of heavy machines is a stone tower. This tower, suitable for a small castle, is oddly out of place with the machinery for rent.

"That castle, I heard it belonged to a man named Kline. I never knew the man but I used to see someone working around this place whenever I drove by. The castle must have been part of a dream he had; why else would a man build a castle? He had all of the land around here and he probably got it cheap because it was so far from anything. I think that Kline must have been a stonemason because when you drove by you could see all types of building stone and flag-stone neatly sorted out into separate piles. He must have had a plan of some kind for his place and it looked like he was organizing it around the tower. He lived in the tower, I heard, but as I said, I didn't know the man. I only saw him from the road and heard him mentioned in the coffee shops and bars. You could come by here and see his old Dodge school bus parked on the property and see Kline, a man in overalls, moving across the land.

One day he was gone. He either died, woke up from his dream, or ran out of money. It's all about the same, isn't it? I drove by and the bus was gone. I had to stop. There was a lot of paper, bills, old letters blowing across the yard. The bus was gone and the whole place had that cold, gone feeling, too. Castles are so impractical in the twentieth century."

About a mile beyond Kline's castle there is a group of buildings built in a long row, railroad-car fashion. This place was once one of the glorious tourist traps along Route 66. The buildings stand behind a tall chain link fence. Their days as roadside attractions are over. Looking closely, though, you can catch a hint of a gaudier, livelier era. Although these buildings are covered with somber, industrial grey paint, you can still see the images of Indian rugs and bold lettering shining through the grey coating. Outside of the imprisoning chain link fence, there is a small escapee of the grey paint fate. A small horno, or beehive-shaped oven, that once must have helped create the "real Indian" atmosphere of this old tourist trading post is now crumbling into dust.

From here, you can look east and see the town of Moriarty in the distance. To the north is a glimpse of the blue Sangre de Cristo Mountains at the end of the long valley. To the right and south, the land and sky sweep away until they meet at the far horizon. The wildness, the vastness, of the land persists despite the small effect of a two-lane strip of asphalt.

MORIARTY

To enter Moriarty from State Road 333, turn right at the stop sign where 333 meets the I-40 exit road. You can see the Rip Griffen Truck Stop from here. Rip Griffen calls his place a travel center, but a truck is a truck is a truck stop.

Trucks dominate the interstate. Trucks rumble by into Moriarty. Trucks, big trucks, eighteen-wheelers, semi-trucks, diesel trucks are everywhere. Because there is no traffic light at the intersection of Moriarty's main street and 333, you may have to wait while several big trucks from I-40 roll past you and onto the asphalt acres of the truck stop. This big truck stop is always busy; one day I counted nineteen trucks lined up and moving slowly into Rip Griffen's.

Moriarty was not named after the wicked professor in the Sherlock Holmes tales. The spelling is the same, though, and once a national organization of Sherlock Holmes aficionados did hold a meeting here, just because of the name. Moriarty was named for Michael Timothy Moriarty, a gentleman from Iowa.

Moriarty's arrival in the Estancia Valley is a typical wanderer's tale. Leaving Iowa in search of relief from a case of chronic arthritis, Moriarty met some enthusiastic boosters of the Santa Fe Railroad, who dazzled the young traveler with tales of New Mexico. The warmer, drier climate would probably be beneficial for an arthritis-sufferer, but one wonders what other public relations gambits were tried on Moriarty by the backers of the railroad. Once in the New Mexico Territory, Moriarty met and traveled with another enthusiastic promoter of the region. This time Moriarty's companion was Edmond Ross, son of the territorial governor. Between Ross and the railroaders from the Santa Fe Company, it is easy to understand why Moriarty decided to stay on in New Mexico.

Both Edmond Ross and Michael Moriarty selected the Estancia Valley for homesteading. Moriarty's health did in fact improve in New Mexico, and he became one of the first permanent residents of the area. When the railroad was built through the valley and a post office was established in 1902, the railroad stop and the post office were named for the gentleman from Iowa.

Moriarty's main street was once U.S. 66, but today there is no trace of the old highway. Instead of the two-lane blacktop, a modern four-lane highway, complete with street lamps and a wide divider, runs the length of Moriarty. But the memory of old 66 is not gone. The Route 66 Shopping Plaza carries the name of the old highway and in the same commercial tradition, it exists to earn a buck from the traveler.

Moriarty's main street contains all of the ingredients of a small town located on a big highway. An insurance agency, a grocery store, a branch bank, a restaurant, and a bar are all present. If you are a celebrity hunter, stop in at the Comedor de Anaya. It is not uncommon for frequent Governor Bruce King, who has a ranch outside of town, or for ex-Governor Toney Anaya, who has family ties in Moriarty, to drop in here for coffee.

The gas stations, cafes, and motels for travelers also line up along this boulevard. This was not always Moriarty's main street. Before I-40, before 66, the town was settled along a street named Central, which is south of I-40 and about a mile down State Road 41, toward the town of Estancia.

Drive south on State Road 41 until you come to a cluster of trees and buildings on the left. You are in the heart of old Moriarty. The buildings are old, strongly built and from a different time. In spite of their age, they have not been abandoned. Citizens of the town are still living here and conducting business out of these sturdy structures.

As late as the mid 1970s, the general store on Central Avenue was open for customers. Stocking a fine array of merchandise that ran the gamut from horse liniment and rock 'n' roll records to clothing and major appliances, it had a little bit of everything. In 1985, the building was destroyed by fire and the store did not reopen.

A businessman by the name of Crossley was instrumental in changing the center of Moriarty from the Central Street location to its present site. Crossley was a far-seeing man and an entrepreneur. In the pre-66 days, Crossley wanted a road. He wanted the business from a major highway for his garage and gas station, but Moriarty at this time was not a main stop on any map. There was a dirt road from the town down into Tijeras Canyon, but it was full of potholes, muddy, and hard to travel. It was little better than no road at all. Since there was no road, the people of Moriarty who set out for Albuquerque drove cross-country, following a fence line or section line south and west until they hit the Tijeras Canyon track.

Crossley wanted something more. He wanted a road from Santa Rosa to Moriarty. Although he didn't know it, he wanted U.S. 66. He lobbied his congressmen and representatives relentlessly. He talked to the governor, the state engineer, the state highway department. At one time, he even drove the engineer over the route he thought this road should take.

Mr. Crossley was finally heard. When the decision to build 66 from Santa Rosa to Moriarty was finalized, it went over the route Crossley had shown to the state engineer. (The story behind this decision is told in part III of this book.) Crossley quickly moved his business from Central Avenue to the side of the proposed road, named his new location Buford after his son, and when the first travelers came down the highway, he was ready to pump their gas and fix their cars. His wife was ready to cook them a meal in their new cafe, and the travelers could also rent a room for the night in the new tourist court. Other businessmen of Moriarty soon followed Mr. Crossley over to the side of Route 66, but Mr. Crossley had a unique angle that set him apart: his was the first gas station in New Mexico that featured a public restroom for travelers.

THE MORIARTY HISTORICAL MUSEUM

If you are interested in Mr. Crossley and the early history of Moriarty, you might consider a visit to the Moriarty Historical Museum. The museum is in the middle of town, on the south side of Main Street, housed in what was once the Moriarty Community Center and Fire Station. The Route 66 wanderer can pull right off Main Street and into the museum parking lot. The hours of the museum are posted on the front door.

This museum is one of those special places that is owned and operated by people, not a bureaucracy. Volunteers from the Moriarty Historical Society are the curators, administrators, and guides. The objects on display are artifacts and possessions of the first settlers of Moriarty. Later citizens of Moriarty have also contributed things that they felt were historic, interesting or important.

The history of Moriarty is largely memory—oral history. The curators of the museum are often the neighbors and descendents of the Moriarty pioneers. They rely on their own memories and those of their friends and relatives to re-create and establish the past. A question to the volunteer on duty can bring forth a string of stories and memories that cannot be put in a display case.

THE PINTO BEAN CAPITAL OF THE WORLD

Moriarty and the Estancia Valley have been called the Pinto Capital of the World. Moriarty folks say that the finest pinto beans on earth come from their fertile valley. This kind of claim is difficult either to prove or disprove but the people of Moriarty probably know what they are talking about; they have been growing pinto beans here for decades.

If you like your pleasures simple: a parade in the sunshine, a good speech by a politician in an election year, a little dancing, a little music, good food, and socializing, then you might want to schedule a visit to the Moriarty Annual International Pinto Bean Fiesta. This communi-

Old timer, Carl Cannon of Moriarty, checks over the chuck wagon in preparation for the Pinto Bean Festival trail ride. Carl came to Moriarty in 1925, before Route 66.

ty event takes placce in Moriarty in the fall, after the pinto bean harvest. Everyone is welcome and it doesn't matter if you like pinto beans or not.

One of the outstanding events of the Bean Fiesta is the trail ride and chuck wagon dinner. The trail ride is strictly BYOH (Bring Your Own Horse). All kinds of horses and all kinds of people show up for this event. You will see weekend riders, show riders, Four H-ers, old-time cowboys, ranchers, babies, and grandmothers. You can also count on seeing a wide variety of horse-drawn conveyances: spring wagons, buckboards, prairie schooners, buggies, and hay wagons. The most important wagon of all, the chuck wagon, will be driven by its owner and builder, Carl Cannon. Carl came to Moriarty in an old slow-speed Ford truck before anyone had even dreamed of Route 66.

The trail ride under the wide sky can be more than just a community picnic. This can be a rare opportunity to get out of your car and see the land from a different perspective. From the back of a horse, you have an opportunity to see this land as Michael Moriarty saw it when he arrived in New Mexico and when the horses and wagons outnumbered the horseless carriages.

THE LOVE HOUSE

One of the most unusual relics of Route 66 east is also the most ordinary-looking. A boarded-up house stands at the side of Main Street toward the eastern end. This house was the home of the Love family, longtime residents of Moriarty. What is unusual about this house is that it is built out of oil cans.

In the thirties when building materials were hard to come by, Mr. Love had an idea. He and his brother-in-law took their truck and drove toward Amarillo. All along the way they stopped and picked up the oil cans discarded by the motorists. When they returned to Moriarty they had a truckful of cans. The next step was to build a house, using the cans like bricks and setting them into cement. When they finished the house, an early recycling project, the Love family moved in. They lived there for more than forty years.

Mr. Love's son, Frank Love, of Albuquerque, remembers the house fondly. "It was a nice house," he says. "Warm in winter, cool in summer, all the qualities of an adobe or a well-built house. You couldn't tell it was made out of oil cans. They were all covered with the cement but sometimes, on the inside, you might notice a little tiny spot on a wall where some of the oil seeped through the cement. It didn't happen often, though."

Look for the house made by Mr. Love when you drive through Moriarty.

SEE RATTLESNAKES LIVE!

If your time has run out in Moriarty and you need to move on, you have two choices. Once again you can hop on the interstate and speed east. You will have no trouble zipping to your destination at sixty-five miles per hour. But if your time is plentiful and your curiosity about Route 66 is still with you, then follow Main Street until you find the sign for State Road 41. Turn north on this road and take the first dirt

Carl Cannon shows us the ruins of John Clair's rattlesnake exhibit. The old pit is visible from the road.

road on the right. This road loops around a neat house and barn and delivers you onto an old road. This old highway was once a section of Route 66. Head east!

"In the old days of Route 66, you could drive down this section of road and see all of those colorful signs put out by the trading post and tourist trap owners. The rattlesnake signs were always pretty flashy; every tourist trap and trading post had a live rattlesnake exhibit. See Rattlesnakes Live! Pit of Terror! Deadly Vipers! You saw those signs all over the Southwest. They were part of the scenery along Route 66.

Down this road, about three miles out of Moriarty, a man named John Clair used to have a tourist stop and a pretty good rattlesnake set-up. Clair was an old carnival hand, an ex-carny, and he had a pretty good idea of how to put on a razzle-dazzle for the tourists. John Clair was an entertainer at heart. He liked an audience and he knew card tricks and jokes and he could spin tales by the hour. Once he quit the carnival his audience became his neighbors and the travelers along Route 66.

Snakes and people. There's something that goes on between snakes and people. Did you ever see that movie the anthropologists made about the little

Carl Cannon points out the faded rattlesnake above the door of John Clair's old Route 66 tourist trap.

chimpanzee and the bag of snakes? It was a bona fide piece of research that took place in a lab somewhere. The anthropologists would give a little chimp a bag with a snake in it. The closed bag would get the best of the little guy's natural curiosity and he would open the bag. Inside there would be a harmless garter snake. The little primate would shriek and close up the bag and run away. In a few minutes though, he would be back, sidling up to the bag, opening it up again to look at the snake. Then he would repeat his performance again, shrieking in fear, leaping away in fright, gibbering and jumping. And in a few minutes he would be back at the bag. He couldn't resist looking in the bag and he couldn't get used to the snake; it always terrorized him and it was a harmless snake.

I think something like that was going on with the tourists and the live rattle-snake attractions along Route 66. Almost every place along the highway had some rattlesnakes to gawk at and people always stopped and looked.

I don't think any of it was for science, either. The tourist trap operators were looking for the money they could get if the tourists stopped. There was good money in gas, postcards, and Cokes. The tourists were looking for a reason to stop their cars and do something besides driving, and rattlesnake exhibits sounded dangerous, exotic, and safe, all at once.

John Clair had a classy rattlesnake pit. Most of the ones you saw along 66 were just a shallow concrete pit sort of dished in the middle to hold a puddle of water. They were usually surrounded by layers of chicken wire so that the tourists couldn't bother the snakes and the snakes couldn't escape. The snakes would just sort of lie around on the concrete, not moving, like snakes tend to do when there is no food or action. The whole situation wasn't exactly a "Pit of Terror." It was sort of boring, but who would complain to the management after being silly enough to fall for a billboard ad? Besides that, it was usually free. Most people would usually just buy a cold pop and drive on, sort of sheepish. They were like that little chimp, though; they couldn't stop themselves from looking if there were snakes to look at.

Little kids seemed to enjoy the snakes the most. They were usually pretty uninhibited unless they had a real strict mother with them. They never saw the chicken wire, they just saw the snakes. They would look and shriek and run away and come back and look again. And the snakes would just lie there, not moving.

But to get back to John Clair. he had a real fancy snake pit painted orange, blue, and white. It had big letters that said "SNAKE PIT" on it and they were so big, you could read them from your car, on the road. His snake pit was about thirty square feet. It was built of concrete, solid, like a box open at the top, like a well or a tank. It was waist-high to a man and little kids had to be lifted up to see into it. There was a nice sunshade over the snake pit so the snakes wouldn't die from the heat and the open top of the pit was covered with a fine mesh screen. There was a strip of steel mesh with narrow slots in it that covered one section of the top. The slots were there so that people could throw coins into the snake pit. I never could figure out why anyone would do that; it certainly didn't have any effect on the snakes. They didn't hiss or coil up or anything. They just lay there and let the coins bounce off of their backs. I sometimes wondered if that was another angle Clair was working with the tourists. He knew a lot about human nature and every winter after the snakes froze up and died, he took an awful lot of money out of that snake pit.

He had to get new snakes every spring. They didn't winter over. When it got warm enough and the snakes came out, the local kids would show up at Clair's place with rattlesnakes in gunny sacks. Clair would buy a new supply of snakes and put them in the pit for the new tourist season. The going rate was a dollar a snake.

During the summer, you could see those kids coming around the tourist traps with snakes in those burlap bags. They would sell snakes to the tourists, when they could. I guess the tourists would kill those rattlesnakes, and cut off

Hondo Marchand and the "Colonel" pose in front of the Longhorn stagecoach, 1968.

the rattles to take home as a souvenir of the West. I can't imagine anyone trying to travel across country with a live or dead rattlesnake in a burlap bag, in a car.

You don't see those rattlesnake places anymore. Maybe the Society for the Prevention of Cruelty to Animals stopped all of that. The operators of the rattlesnake places didn't really take care of the snakes, they just had 'em."

The ruins of John Clair's trading post and rattlesnake attraction are still standing. Look for them on the north side of the road, about three miles out of Moriarty.

THE LONGHORN RANCH

Six miles beyond John Clair's rattlesnake pit is what remains of the Longhorn Ranch. It is on the south side of Interstate 40 although at one time it was right on the side of Route 66, another clear example of the way I-40 and Route 66 cross and recross each other. Of all the tourist traps and attactions along Route 66, the most outstanding, the

The Old West lived again in the Longhorn Ranch's advertising campaigns. This ad appeared in Picturesque New Mexico.

glitziest, and the ritziest was the Longhorn Ranch. The Longhorn Ranch was such a classy tourist trap that it didn't even have any live rattlesnakes. It didn't need them.

After driving across the wide, almost empty landscape of eastern New Mexico, the Longhorn Ranch was a welcome sight. Sometimes as you approached the Longhorn, you might spot a bright red Concord stagecoach pulled by four paint horses, rocking along the side of Route 66. Against the clear red sides of the coach, the brands and the name "The Longhorn Ranch" was picked out in gold. It was a wild and romantic sight and completely incongruous next to the cars on America's famous highway. Few travelers could resist stopping at the ranch, once they had seen the red coach and the paint horses.

The Route 66 travelers didn't have to worry about exits and freeway ramps when they stopped at the Longhorn. The travelers then could simply pull off the highway anywhere within a quarter of a mile of the place and drive right up to the front door. In fact, at the Longhorn

Travelers could simply pull off the highway and drive right up to the door at the Longhorn Ranch, 1954.

you could drive right up to any number of front doors because the ranch was a diversified outfit. At the Longhorn there was a restaurant, bar, and motel, a curio shop and a museum, a garage, gas station, and wrecking service, as well as a working cattle ranch and a hayfield. Most of this operation was presented to the public in a row of store fronts that looked like an old Western town. If it didn't actually look like a real town of the Old West, at least it looked the way everyone thought such a town ought to look: it looked just like a movie set.

The Longhorn Ranch entertained thousands of tourists during its day. Advertisements for it appeared in magazines and newspapers east of the Mississippi and it was the first taste of the "Old West" that many first-time travelers to New Mexico received. The Longhorn Ranch was an institution on Route 66 and many travelers visited it over and over. It was a landmark on the highway between Chicago and Los Angeles.

"I first got acquainted with the Longhorn Ranch before I started traveling and selling up and down Route 66. When the war ended and I landed in Albuquerque, I began to work on my commercial pilot's license, instead of going back to

The Longhorn Bank—busted! 1989.

college. While I was working on my commercial rating, I used to fly out to the Longhorn Ranch for breakfast, on Sundays. It was exciting flying; you had to go over the Sandia Mountains and there was always the possibility that you could be caught in a tricky downdraft and crash. it was a thought that stayed with you on every flight. There was an airstrip at the Longhorn. It was easy to land there and walk over to the coffee shop for breakfast.

In those days the Longhorn Ranch was owned and operated by a man named Erikson. Everyone called him Captain Eric. I don't know too much about the man except that he loved the Old West. Captain Eric filled the Longhorn with his lifetime's collection of antiques, junk, relics, and remnants from the Western past.

The most important collection at the Longhorn, the most interesting, though, was Captain Eric's collection of employees. Most of them looked like they had stepped out of the past and they lent an air of real authenticity to that place. Without them, the Longhorn just wouldn't have been what it was.

Hondo Marchand was the most colorful of all the employees. He was a real working cowboy on the cattle operation of the ranch, but he had other duties, too. Hondo was a slim, wiry man and he looked like everything the word 'cow-boy' implies. With his wide-brimmed Stetson, tall polished boots, and silk neck-scarves, he was the epitome of the old West. Hondo also had a dramatic, black, sweeping mustache that made him look very romantic and exotic in a time when most men were clean-shaven. Oh, Hondo was a fine figure of a cowboy. I heard tell that he was not actually a Westerner at all but was a French Canadian. With the last name of Marchand, maybe that was true. I never knew for sure and Hondo would never tell you the same story twice, if you had the bad manners to ask twice.

The tourists loved Hondo but they rarely saw him working as a cowboy. Whenever a crowd showed up at the Longhorn, Hondo would harness the four paint horses to the red-and-gold Concord stage and take the tourists for rides. The rides cost fifty cents and afterwards you could have your picture taken with Hondo and the stagecoach. I sometimes wonder how many people left the Long-horn with a picture of their family standing next to Hondo and that beautiful stagecoach. There must be thousands of snapshots of Hondo tucked into boxes, drawers, and picture albums all over the country. Wouldn't it be something to see them all?

There was another side to Hondo, too. He was a storyteller, a yarn-spinner, an improviser *par excellence*. At night he would sit in the Longhorn Bar and tell his outrageous tales. The bar at the Longhorn was in keeping with the rest of the place. It had the oldest back bar in the state of New Mexico, a real antique from wilder and woolier days.

The bar was also the showcase for Captain Eric's animal collection. Captain Eric had managed to locate and have stuffed practically every species of animal that ever put down a paw or a hoof west of the Mississippi. There were wildcats, buffalo, bears, bobcats, elk, deer, antelope, prairie dogs, squirrels, and rattle-snakes. There were javelinas, porcupines, armadillos, and coyotes. And not to be boring with the ordinary, Captain Eric also found and had stuffed the derndest collection of two-headed calves, five-legged dogs, and other freaks of nature. These were all displayed in the bar. Hondo had stories for all of those stuffed critters and it was thrilling to hear him describe how he had personally wrestled the mountain lion to the ground and dispatched it with a Barlow knife or how he had cunningly caught the porcupine with a giant pincushion.

Mr. Chamberlain fascinated the tourists, too. He was an older gentleman and he was the proud and careful owner of an authentic prairie schooner and four oxen. Mr. Chamberlain always wore the appropriate Western garb and he would parade his oxen and wagon for the Long Horn's visitors. He would give rides to the tourists and pose patiently for photographs. He was a colorful old gentleman and he lived his part.

Mr. Chamberlain, the proud owner of an authentic prairie schooner, was a major attraction at the Longhorn Ranch, circa 1954.

The Longhorn Ranch Saloon featured the oldest back bar in the state of New Mexico.

Mr. Chamberlain was never out of character or uniform. He always wore a western shirt and a cowboy hat except on his days off. On those days he would exchange the Stetson for a rare and valued St. Louis Cardinals baseball cap. Then he would carefully and meticulously shampoo and de-tick his oxen. Those oxen were as clean as any race horse and probably cleaner than many people. Mr. Chamberlain lent an air of real dignity to the Longhorn.

I remember Margaret, too. She was a tall, handsome woman who worked in the restaurant as a waitress. Other waitresses and fry cooks might drift up and down Route 66 working at one place and then another but Margaret stayed at the Longhorn. She lived in a little apartment in the back and for many years the Longhorn was her home.

Margaret often wore silver earrings in the shape of the Longhorn Ranch brand. It was 2 ⋈ P, which reads as "Two, Lazy Two, P." It always caused a sensation when some visitor would innocently inquire what the letters and the "funny numbers" meant. Margaret would never hesitate to translate the earthy brand, and look the visitor in the eye while she did so. She was quite a lady. I wonder whatever happened to her?

On those Sunday mornings when I flew out to the Long Horn, I used to eat breakfast and chat with Margaret and then walk through the museum. Captain Eric, in his thorough way, had collected everything he could find that had any connection at all to the old West. His museum was extensive. There were two particular sections of it that fascinated me. One was the carriage collection and the other was the slot machines.

Captain Eric had found an example of almost every type of horse-drawn conveyance that had ever been used in the American West. He had his finds restored, repainted, and put into first-class working condition. Every wagon in his museum was ready to be driven; all that was lacking was the harness and the horses and in some cases, he had the correct harness, too.

I looked at those wagons over and over. There were buckboards and beer wagons, freight wagons, chuck wagons, one-horse carriages, and a surrey with the fringe on top. There were hearses, too, one black for adults and one white for children. Both of them had vases at each corner and big glass windows. I never could figure out the windows: Were they for looking out or looking in? And who was supposed to do the looking? And at what?

If a thing had wheels and followed a horse, Captain Eric had one. It didn't matter if it was as small as a dog cart or as tall as a timber wagon, it was there. My favorite in the whole collection, though, didn't have wheels. It was a small red sleigh. It had a complete harness on display with it and the harness was covered with jingle bells. There was every size of bell on that harness from one the size of a hen's egg to one the right size for an elf. It was a beautiful thing but I used to worry about it. No one ever used that sleigh. It was trapped in a dim, high-ceilinged building in the New Mexico desert. Those silvery, jingly bells never got another chance to tinkle and sing in the snowy air. That used to bother me.

After the wagons, I would pay a visit to the slot machines and nickelodeons. In Captain Eric's museum there were all kinds of music boxes, early juke boxes, I guess. There was one that featured a full-sized violin. You dropped a nickel in the slot and then watched through a window as ghostly fingers played that violin. I did it over and over again, trying to figure out the mechanical workings of that thing, trying to put myself in the mind of the man who dreamed it up. I don't remember the music that played, only the appearance of a violin playing without a player. I heard that when they auctioned off the items in the museum that the old violin was purchased by a man from Madrid, New Mexico. He was supposed to have put in the general store there. It was a beautiful and curious piece of machinery, and I still think about it.

There were other mechanical marvels in that collection. There were all kinds of machines that would command the pennies and nickels and dimes out of your pockets. Hardly anything cost a quarter; times were different then. The gypsy fortune-teller would deliberate over her cards and then drop your fortune down a little slot to you. That only cost a penny. For a dime you could choose a song and listen to it on a player piano. The Longhorn Ranch must had made a high profit on all of those machines.

There were slot machines for gambling, too. You couldn't play those because the state laws forbid gambling. Those slot machines just sat there, waiting for a change in the laws that never came. I bet their insides hungered for a dime or a quarter so they could go through their paces, show their stuff and spin their well-oiled wheels again.

Captain Eric wanted everything to work. Occasionally he would stroll through the museum and drop coins in the machines and check them to make sure that everything ran smoothly. Captain Eric was running one of his checks one day and one of the fine old machines balked. The coin dropped down the slot and nothing happened.

A friend of mine was called to the ranch. He was a tinkerer, one of those men who truly understand machines. He arrived at the ranch with his tools and took a look at the old slot machine. When he opened it up, he found the problem. That old machine was clogged with coins. It was jammed with silver, mostly old Mercury-head dimes. That old machine had indigestion from dimes. I've often wished I had those dimes. What a treasure! My friend wished for them too, I know. What a temptation it would have been to be there with a capacious tool box. . . . would have been easy to slip in a handful or two. . . .

It's all gone now. Things change. Route 66 got taken over by the interstate,

*All of the women at the Longhorn Ranch dressed up like 1880s saloon
girls to help celebrate at the Rodeo de Santa Fe.*

the tourists quit stopping at the Longhorn, and it finally closed its doors. It went
through too many owners, in the end. Captain Eric sold it to Walter McCune.
Then there was a long string of absentee owners; that so rarely works. The
Longhorn eventually went into bankruptcy.

There's a sod farm now where the hayfields used to be. You can't drive off of
the highway whenever you want to. There isn't much left of the Longhorn, now.
Everything in it was sold at auction to pay off the debts.

I often think about it. Such good times, such good memories. So many
people stopped at the Long Horn. I missed that auction, wished I could have
gone. Ever wonder how come all the really good stuff, the really fine things
keep ending up at auctions? I wonder who bought that five-legged stuffed dog?"

Pat and Ross Ligon saw the Longhorn Ranch from a different perspective. In the late fifties and early sixties, the Ligons lived and worked
at the Longhorn. Ross was the ranch manager and Pat was the book-

Babe, mascot of the Longhorn Ranch.

keeper and in charge of the day-to-day operations. Route 66 was still the main highway through New Mexico and the Longhorn was still giving all comers a taste of the Old West.

Pat remembers the fun that the staff of the Longhorn Ranch had at the Rodeo de Santa Fe. She recalls, "Everyone would get an elaborate costume together and we would be in the parade for the Rodeo de Santa Fe. It was a big event in Santa Fe then and the whole town turned out for it. All of the waitresses and girls on the ranch would dress up like saloon girls of the 1880s and the men would dress up, too. On the day of the big parade, we would rent a suite of rooms in one of the big hotels in Santa Fe and that would be Longhorn Ranch Headquarters for a day. Hondo would bring the stagecoach and drive it and Mr. Chamberlain would come with the oxen and his prairie schooner. One year we caused such a sensation with our costumes and horses that people thought we were a Hollywood movie crew, in town to make a movie!"

The Ligons found problems, too, on the Longhorn Ranch. Hungry and desperate people traveled down Route 66 and sometimes stopped at the Longhorn, looking for a meal, telling tales of tragedy and hard luck. An

One of the exotic critters at the Longhorn Ranch.

able-bodied man could do odd jobs for a meal, but what could be done for entire hungry families with no money? Neither Pat and Ross nor the Longhorn could finance the poor and desperate. Finally Pat gave standing orders to the kitchen staff that anyone who showed up hungry at the restaurant was to be served a free meal of pancakes. There might not be money for the poor but there would always be pancakes.

Then there was the day the buffalo died. The Longhorn always kept some exotic animals on display for the tourists. There was usually the ranch mascot, Babe, a longhorn steer, a huge brahma bull, and a buffalo, all icons of the Old West. Since the Longhorn wouldn't be the Longhorn without a buffalo, immediate steps were taken to find a replacement buffalo. After telephoning around, a new buffalo calf was found on a game ranch in Oklahoma. Ross and one other man got ready to go to Oklahoma to collect the new buffalo. They took a horse trailer and a pickup truck and set out for a real excursion and a bit of adventure.

In three days the two men returned with the new buffalo calf. They unloaded the calf into the stock corral, tied it, and went into the restaurant for a cup of coffee. They told the people there about the trip

Twin painted and carved totem poles still stand in front of what was once the Longhorn Ranch. The old 2∿P brand is still visible!

and the new buffalo, and went back outside. In a few minutes they were back in Pat's office with alarming news. The buffalo calf had strangled while they were in the restaurant. "We knew that buffaloes had a reputation for being delicate like that and strangling easy," Ross remembers, "but we had tied the calf with care and were only gone long enough to drink a cup of coffee." The buffalo calf had cost $700.

Pat and Ross rose to the occasion, and came up with a plan to salvage the loss. While Ross hung up the carcass and butchered it, Pat called the Albuquerque papers and placed an ad: "Sunday Dinner at the Longhorn Ranch: Tender Buffalo Steak." That Sunday they sold all of the buffalo steak. The Longhorn Ranch didn't lose any money and in a short time there was another buffalo in the stock corral.

During their time at the Longhorn, the Ligons saw several owners come and go. They left the Longhorn Ranch before it closed. Today Pat and Ross are partners on the Ligon Ranch in southwestern New Mexico. Their memories of the Longhorn remain clear and colorful.

Transients sleep in the deserted buildings of the Longhorn Ranch now. The windows are broken and the doors swing open to empty rooms. Weeds grow up in front of the twin totem poles that once framed the entrance to the curio store. Nothing remains of the glamour and fun that were the hallmarks of the Longhorn except the fading brand with the "funny numbers" painted on the door: 2 ⋈ P.

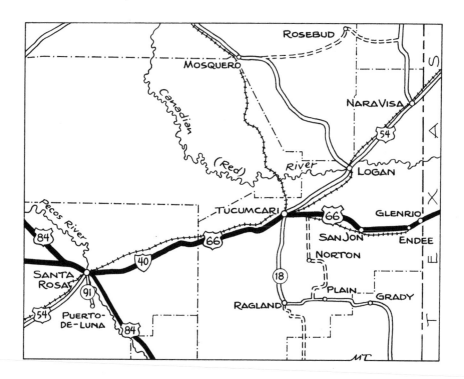

Map 6. *Santa Rosa to Texas (based on* Roads to Cibola, *New Mexico State Highway Commission, 1929).*

10

TO SANTA ROSA

From the Longhorn Ranch, Route 66 ran almost directly east to the Texas-New Mexico border, the same line Interstate 40 now follows. Santa Rosa is the next big town along this straight line, about sixty-six miles away.

The land the highway crosses here is strong and forceful. The Spanish named it the *llano*, which means "plain," and often likened its wide and sweeping character to the sea. Later the land was given other names: prairie, plains, grassland, but none of these words conveys the immensity, the wideness of this land and the wideness of the sky over it.

The force of the land is pervasive. If a car stops beside the road or a hitchhiker waits for a ride, notice that they always choose to stop beside a man-made object. It is as if they don't want to be alone in the landscape, and a highway marker, a stock tank, a billboard, or a bridge across an arroyo will bring some protection or comfort. The land is not flat here but is rippled with small hills and dales. These are not apparent if you gaze across the landscape and let your eyes settle on the horizon. You become conscious of the hills and small draws only when you drive the straight road. Then the highway takes you down into hollows and hides the horizon from you. It lets you climb out and gives you a new view of the *llano*. It seems that nothing fashioned by human hands would be strong enough to interrupt the land and its powerful flow from horizon to horizon.

Man has scratched a few marks in the land, though. Seven miles from the Longhorn is a big rest stop, and two miles beyond that is Clines Corners, a small town that specializes in serving the highway travelers with motels, gas stations, and restaurants. After that only an occasional gas station or highway exit distracts you until you reach Santa Rosa, New Mexico.

Take one of the exits and get off the interstate. Drive onto the frontage road and continue your trip east. Many sections of the frontage road were once Route 66 but without the highway engineer's map, it is difficult to identify every piece of original 66. If you want to do a bit of highway detecting, a few clues will help you decide whether or not you are on the old highway. Look for one of the small concrete bridges that carry the road across an arroyo or stream. When you find one, stop, get out of your car and look for the brass plates on each end of the bridge. One of the plates usually has a bridge number on it and the other will usually have the year the bridge was built and the safe load for that particular structure. The bridge number can be traced but that takes time and archives. The bridge date is the clue you are looking for. If the date is *near* 1938, the year this section of road was named U.S. Route 66, it is likely that you are on a Route 66 highway bridge.

No matter what the date, stopping to look is a great excuse to get out of the car, stretch, and get closer to the land. It also gives you an idea of how small this road across the nation was. It might have been 2,000 miles long, but it was barely fifteen feet wide, and in many places there was no shoulder at all. Compared to the great roaring interstate with its wide lanes, high bridges, smooth ramps, and huge green signs, Route 66 was fragile and puny. The power of this highway was not in the road itself but in what it enabled people to do: travel, escape, change their lives and addresses. Although Steinbeck called this road the Mother Road, and that phrase caught everyone's attention, he also called Route 66 the Road of Flight. Dustbowl farmers, lungers, conmen, and carnival cuties all fled down 66. Babbitts of Main Street, vacationers, traveling salesmen, and Norman Rockwell families all used Route 66, too.

Bridge over the Pecos River, where the two railroads did not *join their rails, contrary to legend.*

SANTA ROSA

If you want to enter Santa Rosa the way the Route 66 travelers used to, leave the Interstate at exit 273. Drive seven tenths of a mile and turn left onto Riverside Road. This narrow lane, once a section of Route 66, winds through a hilly residential section on the edge of Santa Rosa. In the heyday of Route 66 there were fewer houses, fewer cars, fewer people here. This old road will carry you along past the houses and deliver you onto a broader, flatter avenue. The road runs beside the Pecos River, giving you a picturesque view of the old stone railroad bridge spanning the stream.

Legend has it that when the Rock Island Railroad and the Southern Pacific were both building their lines through New Mexico, the companies agreed to merge and form the Rock Island Southern Pacific Line.

The companies began laying track toward Santa Rosa. The Rock Island line came from the east and the Southern Pacific came up from the southwest. The two companies were supposed to meet exactly in the center of the bridge that crosses over the Pecos River. That part is the legend. The two companies did merge and the Southern Pacific Rock Island line did come to Santa Rosa in 1901 but the crews laying the tracks didn't make the bridge rendezvous; they actually met a few yards off the bridge.

Continue on this road, go under the bridge, and turn left onto Coronado Avenue. This is the main street through Santa Rosa and was once called U.S. Route 66.

Santa Rosa is not a town with an ancient past. Although the early Spanish explorers were impressed with the beauty and fertility of the Pecos Valley and named it Eden on their maps, no one came to live in Eden until the middle 1880s. There was no town of Santa Rosa until just before the turn of the century. Santa Rosa's past is only an immediate one; there are now people living here who arrived when Santa Rosa was a dirt road lined with saloons, tents, and a few adobe buildings.

SIDE TRIP TO DON CELSO'S

The first citizen of Santa Rosa was a heavy, round-faced man named Celso Baca. He was a rancher, not a town-builder. He came to this part of the New Mexico Territory to establish a ranch and selected this area because there was water everywhere. Unlike the western portion of New Mexico, the Santa Rosa area is not semi-arid desert. Creeks, springs, lakes, and rivers abound.

Don Celso built a large adobe hacienda and a small adobe chapel dedicated to Santa Rosa de Lima, the first canonized saint of the New World. His small settlement soon became a stopping place for travelers and freight wagons. The stage lines from Las Vegas to nearby Puerta de Luna were routed right by Don Celso's front door, and necessities for people living nearby were dropped off there. The big adobe hacienda with the chapel of Santa Rosa became a well-known landmark.

If you want a small side trip, you can still stop by Don Celso's. Turn south off Coronado Avenue onto State Road 91, proceed through the town of Santa Rosa, past the *new* Church of Saint Rose. Once you are outside of town—and this is surprisingly fast—start looking to your left for a small, crumbling adobe church. Pull over to the side of the

Don Celso Baca's home around 1900. Santa Rosa.

road and park. Behind a rickety barbed-wire fence is the old chapel of Santa Rosa de Lima. The chapel itself looks sad and dilapidated but the cemetery surrounding it seems carefully tended. It is quiet and peaceful here. Across the road is a large, sturdy-looking white building with gables and a shiny tin roof. This is the hacienda that Don Celso built for his family. Its outlines have not changed much since the original construction. It is no longer a home but it is still a stopping place of a kind; a local mortuary uses the building now. Retrace your steps to return to Santa Rosa.

"I used to travel out to Santa Rosa from time to time. I didn't go there as often as I did the towns west of Albuquerque, but I went every once in awhile. I always looked forward to the trip. There would be the long straight drive over the plains and then you'd suddenly be looking into this little green hollow and then you'd drive along the river and slide easily into Santa Rosa.

It wasn't rowdy like Gallup with a bunch of movie crews hollering and laughing and drinking all night. It was nice. It was peaceful.

The people in Santa Rosa were different, too. Small towns have a reputation

La Capilla de Santa Rosa de Lima. Built by Don Celso Baca, circa 1860.

for everyone knowing everyone else's business and whereabouts and this is offensive to some but in Santa Rosa, it wasn't. If I went to make a sales call on a merchant and he wasn't at his store, someone there would go to the door or the window and scan the street. Then they would say 'Well, he drives a '48 DeSoto and it's over there at the coffee shop. Why don't you just step over there and see him?' If they couldn't see his car, they'd tell you where he was planning to go that day, what kind of car he had and I would go and find him. It was easy to do and faster than phoning around. Sometimes I was even told to go and call on people when they were at home eating lunch. No one seemed to mind. I liked that. I always got a pleasant reception in Santa Rosa and I left feeling good."

Santa Rosa is still like this. The citizens of Santa Rosa are still scanning the streets and telling the wanderer how to find their friends and neighbors by where they usually are at 3 p.m., what kind of a car they drive, and what color their house is. It's a small-town kind of ambiance that is supposed to be fading from the American scene, but not

Don Celso Baca's home, 1988.

in Santa Rosa. It may not be life in the fast lane but it's nice, heck, it's charming. You visit in Santa Rosa and feel good about the people, their pride, and their knowledge of their town.

Santa Rosa was not always so calm and peaceful. During the time the two railroad companies were building in the Santa Rosa area, the town boomed with men, money, and jobs. People flocked to Santa Rosa and the dirt-street town of open-front saloons, tents, and adobe shacks grew and grew.

These were the days that brought fame to Nancy, one of Santa Rosa's less-honored residents. Nancy was a gregarious jack donkey whose owner frequented the many saloons in the railroad boom town. This man taught Nancy to drink beer from a glass. After the habit was established, it was easy to teach Nancy to do tricks for beer. Wearing a hat with the crown cut out, Nancy would do a mild hula-hula with his hindquarters or let loose a symphony of internal sounds. Nancy became a favorite in the Santa Rosa saloons. When his owner met with the kind of untimely barroom end that preachers warn us about, Nancy made his living drifting from one open-front saloon to the next, doing tricks for the nutritious beer.

I never met anyone who could tell me the end of this story. Not even the old Peddler heard what happend to Nancy. Not every story in Santa Rosa reached the ears of the travelers going down Route 66.

THE CLUB CAFE

All of the travelers going up and down Route 66 knew about the Club Cafe in Santa Rosa. It was a Route 66 landmark. The Club Cafe is still open, still serving meals to travelers. If you are hungry, stop here for a meal.

The Club Cafe has changed very little over the years; red vinyl booths still line the walls and you can still buy a rubber tomahawk in the gift shop. Located on the north side of Coronado Avenue, near the center of Santa Rosa, it is easy to find. Park in the roomy parking lot and step into history. Ron Chavez, present owner of the Club Cafe, is one of Route 66's most ardent fans.

The first time I ate at the Club Cafe I was with my parents on a summer trip. Our car had no air conditioning and it was hot as New Mexico in August. Even with all of the windows down and our '55 Ford station wagon moving at sixty miles an hour it was so hot that all we could do was sit, drive, and sweat. When we reached Santa Rosa, my father pulled right into the parking lot of the Club Cafe without any of the usual discussion of where we should stop and what kind of food we should eat.

The blast of cold air that hit us when we walked inside was shocking; how could anything be so cold and wonderful after the blazing heat outside? When I slid into the booth, the smooth, cool, red plastic felt so good against the back of my knees that I decided that I would stay in the Club Cafe forever. I was not going home. I was not getting back in the hot car with the scratchy upholstery. I was going to stay in the Club Cafe and never leave.

"When I had to go to Santa Rosa, I would leave Albuquerque before ten, so I could have coffee in Moriarty and lunch at the Club Cafe. It was right on 66 and you could count on seeing some of the other salesmen there at lunchtime and getting the news. They always had good food there. The food was never a surprise. I privately thought of it as '66' food. That was a compliment. It was the best food of that kind you found in eastern New Mexico. It was good solid stuff; chicken-fried steaks, enchiladas, roast beef sandwiches with gravy on white bread, lemon meringue pie. It was always good. Those people at the Club Cafe made you glad you came.

The Club Cafe used a logo that featured a friendly smiling fat man. He just looked well-fed and happy. They put up billboards all over the eastern part of New Mexico with that fat man on them and you couldn't drive east or west without seeing that man by the roadside. They had a Club Cafe in Las Vegas, for awhile, so you'd see the fat man smiling in that part of New Mexico, too. You'd be smiling too when you left the Club Cafe."

ROUTE 66 AND OLDER 66

Whenever Route 66 is mentioned, Santa Rosans will tell you about a road they call "older 66." This road predated U.S. Route 66 and passed through Santa Rosa going west, but it did not follow exactly the same path as Route 66. Older 66 meandered through Santa Rosa and hit Coronado Avenue about where Third Street does today.

If you want to see an aerial photograph of older 66 and Santa Rosa, go to the Rodeo Theater. Rudy Sanchez has these historic photos in his movie house. Sanchez has had his own experiences with Route 66. As a young man, influenced by the movies he saw in the Rodeo Theater and dreams of the Pacific Ocean, he drove a used '55 Chevy to California. It took, in his words, "a hundred gallons of water, six gallons of oil, and I sold the car for $40 when I got there." Rudy Sanchez's career with the moving picture industry got its real start when he returned to Santa Rosa and became associated with the Rodeo Theater.

If you are interested in Route 66 relics and memorabilia, you may want to drive through Santa Rosa and trace the path of Old 66 and older 66. Along the side of the old road, on the east side of Santa Rosa, you can still find examples of the first concrete billboards. Put up before the advent of wooden signs, these squares and rectangles were cast onto boulders standing beside Route 66. The durable and smooth surfaces were painted with advertisements that beguiled motorists as they drove past. These old billboards were practically indestructible. It made no sense to try and tear them down when the road was changed and so they are still standing today.

To trace Route 66 and older 66, take La Pradira Avenue east through Santa Rosa. When you reach a fork in the road, stay on La Pradira and follow the signs directing you to Park Lake. Pass this pretty park with

The author climbs to investigate one of the concrete billboards on old 66. Santa Rosa is in the background.

the municipal swimming hole and continue, now following the signs to Blue Hole. Pass Blue Hole. La Pradira will take a sharp right and straight ahead is a short dirt road passing over a cattleguard. This dirt road is older 66. After the road crosses the cattleguard it becomes a private road. The signs here say "No Trespassing."

Try to ignore the bone jarring ride on this rough road. Look to your left for two concrete rectangles, high up on the rocks, nestled among the mesquite and chaparral. The old signs are empty now. Not a trace remains of a picture or an advertisement. They are pock-marked with bullet scars and some graffiti, yet like old 66, they endure and continue as advertisements for the past.

If you are adventurous and have a thick skin or a suit of armor, you may want to climb up to these old billboards for a closer look. The short walk from the road and the short climb up to the signs will be a nonstop battle with thorns, cockleburrs, cactus, and sticky branches.

The countryside here is more suitable for gazing than walking, and the view from this old stretch of road is splendid. You can see the town of Santa Rosa, the highways that lead into it, and the many pools and lakes nearby.

When you get out of your car, look in the soft dirt at the roadside for deer tracks. Although you are barely out of town, it would not be unusual for you to spot a deer near the road or shyly peeking out from behind the bushes. The squirrels will also greet you with a chirp and a sputter and then scamper away over the boulders. This is a beautiful place to be; half in town, half out, half wild, and half civilized.

To return to Santa Rosa, you must turn around on this road and retrace your steps.

CITY OF LAKES

Santa Rosa is sometimes referred to as the city of Lakes, a condition that has always struck me as unlikely for any city in New Mexico, but the title is appropriate enough here. Wherever you drive in this town you will see signs pointing you toward some lake, spring, creek, pool, or dam. Santa Rosa may be located out on the plains but it isn't in a desert. There is water everywhere.

It was the abundance of water that drew the railroads to Santa Rosa. And it was the railroads that turned Santa Rosa from a stopping place in the road to a railroad town. Then it was the water that drove the railroads away from Santa Rosa.

After the tracks were down and the Southern Pacific and Rock Island lines were joined, the railroad executives decided that Santa Rosa would be the best place to establish a big roundhouse and maintenance yard. It looked like the future of little Santa Rosa was assured. Railroads practically guaranteed prosperity.

The prosperity didn't last much longer than it took to build the roundhouse. All of that water which so attracted the railroad companies was, in the words of Santa Rosans, "mineral." It was so "mineral" that when it was pumped into the boilers of the railroad engines and heated to steam, it left a heavy gypsum deposit. The gypsum fouled up the internal workings of the steam engines and rendered them useless. The abundant water of Santa Rosa was exactly the wrong chemical composition for the locomotives. Before you could say "Culligan!" the railroad companies closed down their operation in Santa Rosa and moved

The Armstrong house of Santa Rosa was built with sandstone blocks salvaged from the old roundhouse.

their headquarters and maintenance yards to Tucumcari. The water there was less "mineral" and suited the steam locomotives just fine.

Without the railroad, Santa Rosa became less wild and less woolly. The city fathers took another, different look at their town and started to make changes. They decided that there was no need for a street full of saloons and they passed a law declaring that only one saloon could operate in town. Then Santa Rosa became even less wilder and woollier. One can only hope that the last saloon in Santa Rosa was one that had a regular four-legged customer named Nancy.

THE ROUNDHOUSE HOUSE

Without maintenance yards at Santa Rosa, there was no need for the roundhouse. The sandstone block structure was dismantled and the blocks were carried to the corner of Sixth Street and Capitan, where

Rudolph Johnson in the doorway of the old Ilfeld warehouse. Mr. Johnson, current owner of the place, has filled it with relics of Santa Rosa's history.

they were used to build a large two-story house for the manager of the lumberyard, Mr. Humphreys. The Humphreys' house was spacious and featured a complete basement, attic, kitchen, and bedrooms as well as a thirty-foot living room with a ten-foot ceiling. The Humphrey house, which still stands at the corner of Sixth Street and Capitan, is said to look just as it did during the early part of the century. All alterations and remodeling have been restricted to the inside.

The handsome tan block home is now owned by Roy Armstrong, a retired rancher from House, New Mexico. He moved his family to Santa Rosa when it was time for his children to attend "regular" school. He bought the house on the corner of Capitan and Sixth in 1951. He and his daughter Rosalie are still calling the Roundhouse house their home.

As you drive through Santa Rosa, heading east, you may spot another imposing sandstone block building down by the railroad tracks, near the center of town. This is the old Ilfeld warehouse. You can easily identify this building by the large sign in front that reads "Rudolph Johnson."

"That big old warehouse? I remember when it belonged to the Ilfelds. They came to New Mexico early on and started trading. They weren't just storekeepers, they were merchants. They bought and sold everything and that was their motto: 'Wholesalers of Everything.' They painted that on the front of their warehouses and it was true. Everything anyone could want, the necessities of life, the Ilfelds had in their warehouses. They had warehouses all over the state; theirs was a big business. Sometimes the biggest place in town was the Ilfeld Warehouse. All of their warehouses were big, like this one and most of them were close to the railroad tracks. Seems like every town I carried my order book into had an Ilfeld Warehouse. I remember one in Albuquerque, Gallup, Las Vegas, and Magdalena. They had them in a lot of other places, too: smalltowns in New Mexico where you would think no business could flourish would have a big Ilfeld establishment."

The Ilfeld Warehouse in Santa Rosa is impressive. Built of sandstone blocks and wood, it is roughly fifty feet wide, a hundred feet long, and thirty-five feet tall. It has a full basement complete with a potato chute, a half-ton scale, a cedar-lined tobacco room, and the original hydraulic elevator. In its day, this warehouse must have been an awesome sight. The Ilfelds were counted on to carry everything needed to farm, ranch, or simply get along. This cavernous building was at one time filled with tools, guns, ammunition, dry goods, foodstuffs, household necessities and luxuries as well as specialty items needed by farmers and ranchers.

Today the Ilfelds are no longer in business and the building is owned by Rudolph Johnson. But the warehouse is not empty. Today the Ilfeld Warehouse is filled with an amazing variety of antiques and memorabilia Johnson has collected. From the first electric stove of Santa Rosa to the souvenir programs from the high school rodeo, Rudolph Johnson collected them all. The warehouse contains a lifetime of business and living in Santa Rosa.

Rudolph Johnson knew Route 66. As the Texaco distributor in the Santa Rosa area, Johnson's business pumped hundreds of gallons of gasoline into the trucks and cars wheeling down Route 66. At one time he figured that 88 percent of Santa Rosa's economy came from the Route 66 traffic.

In the thirties, Route 66 contributed to Rudolph Johnson's own economy, too. When construction crews were paving Route 66 between Santa

Rosa and Tucumcari, Johnson got a job driving the paver or lay-down machine. It was hot, smelly work but a job was a job. The pay was ninety cents an hour and one time he worked twenty-three hours straight. It was amazing in the thirties and for different reasons, it is amazing today.

There are many more people in Santa Rosa with stories and memories about Route 66. If you are interested, go and find some. No doubt you will hear something I did not. You might meet someone the Peddler never knew. Memories of Route 66 are waiting for you in Santa Rosa.

Leave Santa Rosa on Coronado Avenue, heading east. In a short time the street will give way to the interstate and you will be headed out to Tucumcari.

TUCUMCARI TO TEXAS

TUCUMCARI

Leave Santa Rosa for Tucumcari, going east. Although you can drive
out of Santa Rosa on Coronado Avenue and take this old strip of 66 a
little ways out of town, you will eventually end up at a barbed-wire
fence marking private property and a dead end. In order to get to
Tucumcari, you will have to travel the interstate for a few miles.

This stretch between the two old railroad towns was the last leg of
a long day's drive for many travelers on Route 66. Today the last leg is
broken up by the signs and exits along the interstate announcing Los
Tanos, Cuervo, Newkirk, Montoya, and Palomas. These tiny towns
and villages all sprang up between 1901 and 1902 as the railroad
threaded itself between Santa Rosa and Tucumcari.

If you are still in the mood for wandering and exploring, get off the
interstate and visit Montoya or Cuervo or Newkirk. They are waiting
for you. Cruise down the main street of one of these little towns and
try to see it as a bustling boom town. It was once full of people and
activity. Stroll through the cemetery and read the tombstones. Sometimes you can catch a glimpse of a town's unique continuity, history,
or tragedy during a graveyard tour. Who knows what awaits the wan-

---

Bridge on the frontage road between Tucumcari and Santa Rosa. A vestige of Route 66.

derer in these quiet and dusty places? Go and see. The interstate will still be there when you have finished.

At Montoya, for example, Route 66 was not abandoned completely but was converted to a frontage road. The little concrete bridge a mile or so along the frontage road is numbered 1757 and was built in 1936. There is nothing unique about this particular Route 66 bridgelet except it has both its number plaque and date plaque intact. If you cruise along this old highway, you might find another like it.

The road from Santa Rosa to Tucumcari stretches its sixty miles across the *llano*. At the end of the day, this last sixty miles can seem endless. If you know "The Tucumcari Song" you can start singing it and soon you'll be agreeing with it, too:

> Tucumcari, Tucumcari,
> I just gotta get home!
> Sixteen miles to Tucumcari,
> And I'll never more roam!

Brass identification plaques set into either end of the old bridge.

Seven miles outside of Tucumcari, the road signs advertising "the town two blocks wide and two miles long" start to show up in force. Watch for interstate exit 329 so you can get off and drive into Tucumcari following the route of U.S. 66, a very pleasant way to approach town. This road takes you a short jaunt through the countryside and shows you that Tucumcari is an agricultural town surrounded by farms and ranches.

KID ON A HORSE

"I used to drive towards Tucumcari watching the plains for movement. It wasn't uncommon to see cowboys working the cattle as you drove by on Route 66. Sometimes those cowboys you saw were so young looking, or at least they looked small—just a boy on a horse all alone on the *llano*. I wondered about those kids; did they grow up and stay cowboys or did they get their diplomas and beat it down Route 66, leaving the horses and cattle and rough work, for good? Most people start a career when they're half grown at twenty but if you worked as a kid 'til you were twenty and then went on working it seems that you get a lifetime-and-a-half at your job, and one ought to be enough!"

Bill Bonds was one of those small cowboys out on the *llano* on a horse. Born in Tucumcari, Bonds spent his boyhood in halves: Half the time he lived in town with his mother, the other he spent with George and Esther Barton on the Barton Ranch. The Bartons were his second family and the Barton Ranch was his second home.

The Barton Ranch combined a dairy and a farming operation along with the cattle. Young Bill turned his hand to every kind of work. He spent hours on horseback, hours under the wide New Mexico sky. He learned to work alone, to be independent, to accept the responsibility when others were counting on him.

School and the army took Bill Bonds away from Tucumcari. He went to war, he went to school, and he never went back except to visit. Today the soft-spoken Bonds is a CPA in Albuquerque, a success in his career, a father and a grandfather. But Bill Bonds is still a Tucumcari cowboy, a kid on a horse out on the New Mexico *llano*. In his office in metropolitan Albuquerque, Bonds has a picture of a small white-faced calf, hunkered down by some yuccas, under a wide sky.

When asked about the picture, Bill Bonds replies, "When I look at

Tucumcari's main street, 1990. Route 66 is not forgotten: the curio shops are still open, waiting for motorists.

that painting, I see my boyhood. I spent so many hours on a horse looking after cattle. You would often see the little calves lying down, just watching as you rode by. There was a certain distance between you and the calf and if you came too close, the calf would get up. You had invaded his space, as they say today. You hardly ever saw a single calf like that, all alone. They were usually with their mamas. Sometimes, though, you would see a cow with several calves around her; cows sort of babysit for each other. The little calves bunch around one cow and the other mothers go off alone for awhile. If you find one calf alone like that, something usually happened to his mother. You have to get him up in front of you on your horse and take him home. When I look at that picture, that's what I see. I see my boyhood. If there was a fire in the office and I could take only one thing out, it would be that picture."

Bill Bonds is approaching his retirement. He has no plans to live in Tucumcari. He only returns to that town to visit his mother. Route 66 took Bill Bonds away from his hometown but it couldn't take the kid on the horse off the *llano*.

Almost as soon as you are free of the interstate, brown-and-white shield-shaped signs begin to pop up along the roadside and let you know that you are following historic Route 66. This wide road with the double lanes and concrete dividers doesn't look like narrow old 66, but the way it zooms straight through Tucumcari makes you know it must be.

In the halcyon days of Route 66, Tucumcari, New Mexico *was* known as the town two blocks wide and two miles long. Route 66 went right through the heart of town and that phrase described the concentration of tourist courts, restaurants, gas stations, and curio shops that catered to the motorists traveling the highway. It was a cliché, of course; there was more to Tucumcari than that. Tucumcari was a railroad town, and a supply center for farmers and ranchers long before Route 66 stretched its black ribbon of asphalt out from the Texas border.

Although Tucumcari is not just a city of innkeepers, it is a town with its share of inns. Drive up and down the main street, Tucumcari Avenue, and what strikes you is the many motels, tourist courts, inns, and hotels. A few of these look new, local outposts of national companies, but many of them were built in the days when Tucumcari was a natural overnight stop on Route 66 whether you were driving east out of Gallup or west from Amarillo.

Some of these motels have interesting names like the Blue Swallow or the Aruba but most of them have a name and a big sign that evokes the Old West. You can see the Apache, the Buckaroo, the Cactus, the Lasso, and the Palamino, just to name a few. All of the signs are decorated with horses, cowboys, Indians, cactus, sagebrush, branding irons, six-shooters, and lariats. The romance of the Old West did not die in Tucumcari.

Interstate 40 bypasses Tucumcari to the south, but it does not obscure the view of the Tucumcari Mountain rising out of the *llano* in an abrupt, steep bluff. The town got its name from this mountain and also became saddled with an improbable but clever legend that is supposed to explain the meaning of Tucumcari. This is a legend that seems to gloss over facts very lightly but is strong on drama.

The tale begins with four Indians, supposedly Apache, named Wautonomah, Tocom, Tonapon, and Kari. Tocom and Tonapon were rivals for the hand of the beautiful maiden, Kari. (In legends, there are few homely maidens.) Kari favored Tocom over Tonapon. The two rivals became involved in a duel to the death and Tocom was the loser. The distraught and bloodthirsty Kari then murdered Tonapon and committed suicide. Kari's father, Wautonomah, equally distraught by the deaths of the three young people, then stabbed himself to death while crying out "Tocom! Kari! Tocom! Kari!" Thus the town acquired its name.

This tale is credited to Geronimo, a man of above average intelligence. It might be that he was also a man with a well-developed sense of humor who was going to see just how gullible people could be. In reality, this legend with all of its blood and melodrama might be more at home on a Wagnerian opera stage than the plains of Tucumcari.

Such legends aside, Tucumcari did acquire its name from nearby Tucumcari Mountain. The plain fact about the mountain is that it is in Comanche, not Apache, territory. The Comanche Indians were known to have used this high ground for both signal fires and surprise attacks. There are words in the Comanche language concerning ambushes and signals that do in fact sound like "Tucumcari." There might not be any words that sound like Wautonomah.

The Chamber of Commerce of Greater Tucumcari takes a neutral stand on the origin of the town name. They sensibly would rather tell you about the annual Tucumcari Pinata Festival, the Tucumcari Historical Museum or any of the businesses in their town.

"I never did much business in Tucumcari. I sold hard goods and there weren't too many customers up there. I liked to call on Harry Garrison, though. After he quit the restaurant business and retired, he had a little furniture and second-hand store down by the railroad station. I would go in there with my order book ready and come out with it empty and would have spent three hours in there talking to him about the old days of Tucumcari and looking through the old phonograph records and books that people sold to him.

He kept a pair of yellow-and-black cowboy boots hanging up behind the counter. They were elegant-looking boots, looked handmade, custom-made. Worked into the tall shaft of each boot was a pair of crossed six guns; I'd never seen anything like them. I asked Harry about them and he just let loose with that big laugh of his and said "So you like my 'Two Gun' boots! I ain't gonna sell 'em. I like to keep 'em around.' Then he started whistling that old song that made him famous, stopped in the middle of it, and got busy behind the counter. He was looking through a stack of papers and pretty soon he pulled out the one he wanted and handed it to me. It was a picture of him wearing those tall boots, a cowboy hat, and a set of six-guns. He was standing in front of his restaurant: Two-Gun Harry of Tucumcari. 'Two-Gun, Two-Gun,' he said softly. 'I sure enjoyed those days.' "

Those days were the days at the end of the forties. Those were the days when Harry Garrison was not a furniture store owner but the flamboyant, ebullient man made famous by Dorothy Shay in the hit song, "Two-Gun Harry from Tucumcari." Today there may not be many

1948 snapshot showing Harry Garrison's restaurant at the time the song "Two-Gun Harry from Tucumcari" was written.

people who know where Tucumcari, New Mexico is, but there are thousands who have heard the song about Two-Gun Harry, a bow-legged, gun-toting cowboy with a lovesick girlfriend.

Harry Garrison was never a working cowboy. He owned Harry's Lunch, a post-World War II version of a fast-food restaurant located a step or two across from the railroad station in Tucumcari. He was a colorful, gregarious man, a self-appointed ambassador to the world from Tucumcari. He met every arriving passenger train dressed up in showy Western clothing, wearing his twin pearl-handled six-guns. Once he had attracted the attention of the passengers on the trains, he would escort them across the street to his restaurant. He was a dramatic public relations act for Harry's Lunch.

One day, Dorothy Shay, a popular singer known as the Park Avenue Hillbilly, stepped off the train in Tucumcari. Harry was there as usual, tall, handsome, and charming, in his full Western regalia. He escorted

Reverse of the 1948 snapshot. In Garrison's handwriting, "This is the original look of the cafe when the song was written."

the singer across the street to the restaurant and she later wrote a song about falling in love with a Tucumcari cowboy. A lot of fantasy can be packed into a twenty-five minute layover, burger, and fries.

After Dorothy Shay's song became a hit, many travelers pulled off Route 66 and into Tucumcari feeling like they knew something about the place. After all, they had just driven across a country where every radio station was playing the song about the Tucumcari cowboy and his love. Now they were in his hometown, scene of the musical romance. The actual facts about Harry and Dorothy's short meeting were irrelevant.

The fame of Two-Gun Harry became irrelevant, too. The passenger trains quit stopping in Tucumcari, Harry closed the business and retired, and the popular song turned into a golden oldie. Only a few people in Tucumcari remember the man, the times, and the song.

Harry died in 1987. He left his business and the buildings by the

Photo of Two-Gun Harry Harrison. A rare shot of the man in the song who went on to become President of the New Mexico Restaurant Association.

railroad tracks to his friend, Frances Chacon. Frances still opens the business on most afternoons. You can go down to the old railroad station and a bit to the west of it, find the furniture store with the plants filling the front windows. If Frances is not busy with a customer she might show you an old 78 record, an original recording of Harry's song. She might tell you stories about Harry, his open-handed generosity, his love of people, his sense of fun, and the many sandwiches he cooked and she served at Harry's Lunch. So,

> If you're ever traveling west,
> I'd wish you'd give my best
> To a man whose name is Two-Gun Harry.
> When the train gets into town,
> You'll see him hangin' round
> In a station they call Tucumcari . . .

The original 78 rpm record featuring the hit song by Dorothy Shay.

THE TUCUMCARI HISTORICAL MUSEUM AND
RESEARCH INSTITUTE

If you need or want a refresher course in the Reality of the Old West, drive four blocks north of Tucumcari Avenue (Route 66) on Adams Street to the Tucumcari Historical Museum. This place is maintained by the Tucumcari Historical Research Institute, which, according to the organization's brochure, is "dedicated to preserving the early Southwest. . . ." These people are a definite success at what they do. They have not only collected objects and artifacts concerning all facets of life in the Southwest, but they have assembled them in such a way that the museum visitor can see at once the setting in which the objects were used.

You don't see just an early hospital bed or a doctor's case, for example; you're presented an entire hospital room complete with many ob-

Harry Garrison's cafe in the 1950s. This was the heyday of Mr. Garrison's place.

jects from the days of frontier doctors. You are not asked to look at an old Victrola all by itself in a glass case; you are treated to the sight of an early American parlor that contained such a Victrola. You may also look at pioneer kitchens, an early post office, a schoolroom, a fire station, and a room dedicated to ranch life. This is a museum where they provide the setting and the clues and you provide the imagination to place yourself back in time, in the Old West.

The Old West may be enticing to many tourists but the Tucumcari Chamber of Commerce believes firmly in the New West. When Route 66 streamed through Tucumcari the Chamber of Commerce took the highway very seriously. In many ways that highway was the lifeblood of the Tucumcari business sector. It brought the customers to town and a degree of prosperity to the townspeople.

TUCUMCARI TO THE TEXAS BORDER

But Route 66 had its drawbacks, too. The forty miles from Tucumcari to Texas was a hazardous road that could take customers away from Tucumcari in a permanent way.

If a flat interrupts your kicks on Route 66, just pull over. 1940.

"Route 66 between Tucumcari and the border—what a terrible road that was. It was full of big potholes, narrow, and in places it didn't have a shoulder. Hell, in some places it didn't even have a center line. Driving across that monotonous flat country it was real easy to quit paying attention and drop a wheel into one of those holes. Then you'd be in a fight with a ton-and-a-half of car trying to get it back in the right lane. A lot of drivers trying to make Tucumcari, driving too long, driving too far, would fall asleep on that stretch of road and lose control of their cars on that terrible road. I wonder why they never maintained it? They used to say that you were only six inches and a cigarette paper away from Death on Route 66."

Damon Kvols of Tucumcari wanted to do something about that "terrible road." In the sixties, Kvols was president of the Tucumcari Chamber of Commerce. He lobbied, petitioned, testified, and badgered various highway authorities in an attempt to have Route 66 widened and made safer. Like Mr. Crossley of Moriarty before him, Kvols wanted a better road. Like Mr. Crossley he also fought a determined battle, explaining the need to politicians and bureaucrats in Santa Fe. It was a long battle and Damon Kvols never saw the end of it. He was killed in a car wreck on Route 66, east of Tucumcari. He died without seeing the wider, safer Interstate 40 replace hazardous Route 66.

Tucumcari named a city park for Damon Kvols, honoring the man who tried to change Route 66. It's easy to find on the east side of town; the road that was once Route 66 goes right by it.

If you like al fresco dining, take a picnic lunch to the Damon Kvols Park. It has trees and picnic tables as well as a playground with swings and a slide. Play in the sun or lounge in the shade and before you drink the last of your lemonade, drink a toast to Mr. Kvols and Route 66.

"Come on, kid. We've got to get out of here if we want to get home before dark. There's nothing up the road between here and the border but Logan. It's a nice town, all right, but I know you just want to visit that bar up there called 'The Road to Ruin.' I'm not being responsible for that! I figure you're on your own road to ruin, fooling around with me and all of the ghosts of old Route 66. You've spent enough time in bars, anyway. If we hurry, we can get back to the La Posada by five o'clock."

PART III

HANNETT'S JOKE

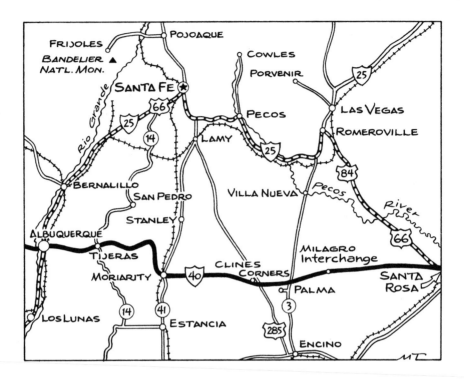

Map 7. *Original old Route 66 (based on* Roads to Cibola, *New Mexico State Highway Commission, 1929).*

FALSE EPILOGUE

Back at the La Posada, the old Peddler sank into an easy chair in the lobby and waited for a drink. People around us chatted and laughed, ice tinkled in glasses, and the cocktail hour was underway. It had been a long drive home.

You'll have to go to Santa Fe tomorrow, without me," he said. "I'm wore out. I can't keep up this galivanting around. I need to find a comfortable chair and sit in the sun. I'm an old man."The words had a pathetic ring but the Peddler's eyes were shining with mischief. The hand that held the drink and had gripped the steering wheel from Tucumcari to Albuquerque was perfectly steady.

I knew I was being set up but I didn't know for what. I went ahead and asked the question the Peddler was waiting for. "Why would I want to go to Santa Fe? I have to work on this Route 66 book."

"Oh," he said innocently, "Didn't you know Route 66 used to go through Santa Fe? But it was 'way before my time, in the early twenties; you'll have to find out about it yourself."

"You just don't want to go to Santa Fe," I accused him. "All those Beautiful people. All those fine Santa Fe women with their long, flowing skirts. All those tourists."

"You're right," he said. "I prefer short skirts. But we could go to the library at the University of New Mexico. You could find the map that

Route 66-85 near Algodones between Santa Fe and Albuquerque. From New Mexico Highway Journal, 1930.

shows Route 66 going through Santa Fe and I could sit in the patio in the sun. No tourists there. Just pretty students."

"I'll pick you up here in the morning," I said with resignation.

The Peddler raised his glass. "To Santa Fe!" he said. "To Santa Fe and Route 66!"

HANNETT'S JOKE

The Peddler was right. Route 66 did go through Santa Fe at one time. It is a tale of power and politicians and so peculiarly New Mexican.

The main highway through New Mexico used to go from Tucumcari to Santa Rosa, Santa Rosa to Romeroville, then down through Santa Fe to Albuqueruque, south to Los Lunas, back up and west to Correo, and then on to Grants, Gallup, and the Arizona border. This was the original path of Route 66 until 1926.

In that year the governor of New Mexico, A.T. Hannett, was running for re-election. Through various incidents of double-dealing or perhaps just plain bad politics, Hannett lost the race. Annoyed with the poli-

ticos in Santa Fe, who he felt had caused his defeat, Hannett decided to teach them a lesson. He would be governor until the new man, Richard Dillon, took the oath of office in January. He still had some time.

Hannett called the district highway engineer and told him to gather up men and equipment and start building a road from Santa Rosa to Moriarty. The new road would allow travelers to cross New Mexico by going through Santa Rosa, Moriarty, and Tijeras Canyon to Albuquerque, completely bypassing Santa Fe, the Santa Fe business community, and the Santa Fe politicians. He was the governor, he still held office and by George, he would have a road bypassing those politicians in Santa Fe.

The state engineer, E.B. Bail, swung into action and began organizing the project. It might be his last one—he was sure to be out of a job when the new governor took office, and besides he knew where the road should be built—Mr. Crossley of Moriarty had once driven him over the cross-country route.

After Bail had assembled the work crews, only thirty-one days remained in which to build a road sixty-nine miles long. There would be no time off, not even for Christmas. The men in the crews didn't care; they knew when a new administration came to power in Santa Fe, that most of them would be out of work, anyway. They could rest then. Besides, they admired the guts and audacity of Hannett. They considered his project a huge joke and they rose to the challenge with enthusiasm.

Construction got under way with the men divided into two crews. One group started at Santa Rosa and worked west, while the other group began in Moriarty and worked east. It was hard work. The road passed through heavy stands of scrubby piñon and juniper. The December weather hindered the crews with rain and snow, and the work day was determined by the short daylight hours. Still, the roads grew toward each other.

There was opposition. Although Governor Hannett did have the power to order construction, it was not an entirely popular decision. Machinery was sabotaged repeatedly until the men began to sleep in the open to guard it. The work continued.

The road forged across the country, across public and private property alike. There was no time to dicker with property owners about purchased right-of-ways. Fences were cut and the land was surveyed, graded, smoothed, and graveled. No one tried by legal means of courts and injunction to stop or delay the road. Hannett's joke progressed.

When the new governor was sworn in, the road was still not completed. On his first day in office, the new governor sent an engineer to halt the work but a freak turn in the weather prevented his arrival. Hannett's joke was completed and travelers were spinning down the gravel track by the time the engineer reached the work site. Hannett had his road and his joke.

Hannett often pointed out what a service he had done for travelers. By passing Santa Fe, he shaved more than ninety miles off the trip across New Mexico and got the westbound motorists to Gallup that much faster: Hannett was the ex-mayor of Gallup, too. A real boon to the traveler, old Route 66.

INDEX